IF YOU BELIEVE YOU CAN HEAL YOURSELF YOU CAN

7 STEPS TO OPTIMAL HEALTH AND HAPPINESS = VITALITY

UNDERSTAND HOW TO ACHIEVE OVERALL HEALTH AND HAPPINESS = VITALITY

Vitality: from Latin vitalitas, from vitalis "pertaining to life" the state of being strong and active, The capacity to live, grow, or develop. Synonyms: liveliness, life, energy, spirit, spiritedness, high-spiritedness, vivacity, exuberance, buoyancy, bounce, vibrancy, verve, vim, pep, zest, zestfulness, sparkle, spark, effervescence, dynamism, passion, fire, vigour, ardour, zeal, relish, gusto, push, drive

Would you like to live with Vitality, to know how it feels to live with Vitality? Be Curious, ASK and live the life you were meant to live.

This Book is dedicated:

For Wayne, we "fit", you complete me. Thank the universe for mini-tabs! Thank you for being my guinea pig I am always thankful and appreciative you that will give it a try and I am so proud of the changes you have made, thank you for coming on my journey with me, for getting on the crazy train.

Acknowledgments

Thank you to my family, without whom I would not have had the belief that I could be and do anything and that I was never a failure as long as I just tried and did the best I could. Mum you were the one who made me question and realise that medication wasn't always the answer and there were always alternatives. To Nu-Nu who showed me that age was just a number and although we age chronologically we don't have to get old, I love and miss you

Thank you to all my friends, those who always believed in me particularly the times when I didn't believe in myself, you all know who you are but special thanks to Caroline Langan, Katy Robinson and Christine Walker. Thank you to my NSP team and family, you all rock! To my wonderful Theta Healing ® teacher Pippa King, the amazing ladies I trained with Amy, Allison, Denise, Aaron and Susan for all your guidance and support.

The EBC1 group, for your support, feedback, input and for keeping me accountable, particularly in writing and finishing this book, the first of many. A special thanks to Sally Marshall who introduced me to the group and inspired me and showed me that writing a book was easier than I thought as Sally always says "If you want it badly enough, you will find a way" – thanks for showing me the way.

And last but not least a big thank you to Wayne Scholtz for your patience. Thank you for the cover design, and help with all the fabulous graphics and "techy stuff"

SMILE

Always smile – do you know what happens when you smile?
You raise your vibration.

Life is meant to be enjoyed not endured!!

Pass your smile on, it costs you nothing and may just make someone else's day

Kerry is a Holistic Entrepreneur: her love, life, work and spirituality are not separate.

Kerry qualified with a Total Immersion Diploma in 2012, including Advanced Personal Trainer, GP and Exercise Referral, Pilates, Sports Nutrition and Nutrition for Weigh Management and then went on to complete a Diploma in Nutritional Therapy and Clinical Nutrition, Nutrition for Allergies and Intolerances in 2012, attended a basic Gerson Therapy Training Course and is currently training as a Naturopath and Theta Healer having completed the basic course and continuing with her training as a Theta Healer ®.

Kerry runs her own thriving online and Kent-based business. Her clients are open-minded people and come to her primarily seeking help with chronic fatigue, digestive issues and chronic pain, and they are tired of taking medication and want natural solutions and long to be in control of their health once and for all - improving their energy levels, digestive health and achieving optimal health – or a combination of these. Kerry's works with her clients via natural solutions to help activate the body's own natural healing pathways.

Kerry also offers Coaching and Support to open minded Entrepreneurs looking for financial independence, personal freedom, and the ability to choose how they spend their time each day, Kerry's helps by creating an individual plan to help clients realise the life they dreamt about when starting their business.

The ThetaHealing® Technique is a meditation training technique utilizing a spiritual philosophy for improvement and evolvement of *mind, body* and *spirit*.

CONTENTS

Introduction	7
STEP 1: Mind Your Mind - Thoughts and emotions	15
STEP 2: Nourish Your Body and Mind - Nutrition	35
STEP 2.1: Hydration	65
STEP 3: Taming the Toxic Overload	69
STEP 4: Movement	75
STEP 5: Breathing	77
STEP 6: Stay Healthy, Sleep Well	79
STEP 7: Stress	83
Vitality+K 7 Step System	91
Conclusion	95
Setting Health Goals	97
Additional Rules to Live By	99
Vitality+K 3 Day Kick-start	103
Resources	111
Downloads	113
A message from Kerry	115

INTRODUCTION
WHO I AM – MY STORY

I have been healing my body with food - REAL food, learning how to live an organic and toxic free lifestyle as best I can and exploring mind-body-spirit health. A number of years ago, I ended up sick, tired and stressed, prescribed with a number of medications which I took for a while in the hopes of a "quick fix" but none of them solved the issues I was having. When I discovered one of them was an anti-psychotic medication which was prescribed for stress, I knew there had to be a better way. I was fortunate to work for myself but I was not very effective during my working hours and I was not able to enjoy my time off.

I made a lot of changes in my life, I changed what I ate and when I ate, I changed the type of exercise I did and I saw great results, I had fewer symptoms and those that I had reduced in severity and my health improved but there was still something missing. It is not until I changed all areas of my life, my thoughts, beliefs and behaviours that things really started to change – I got much healthier and happier! I was told that I had too much stress in my life, that was not helpful – I knew I was stressed I just did not know what I could do about it, it was only when I realised I could manage the stress and found a number of techniques which we will explore, it was by managing the stress not necessarily reducing the amount of stress but reducing the effects of stress in my life that things really started to shift and change.

You may be wondering who I am and why I have written a book but I truly believe that we all have a book in us - we are all unique and we all have a story to tell and to share, if this helps one other person or it gets you thinking about your health, understanding that you have choices, whether you choose conventional medicine, alternative therapies or complimentary therapies – there are always ways you can improve your health – I encourage you to have hope, just decide, ask and be curious.

I was raised on a farm and grew up during a war which had its stressful times but as a whole I remember my childhood as a happy carefree time. At this point in my journey I prefer to look at the positive rather than the negative aspects of growing up although as we will explore later, these are the foundation of our beliefs, thought and behaviours. I will always be a farm and outdoor girl at heart and still prefer to be bare foot – although this can be a bit chilly in the winter as we now live in the UK, much colder than where I grew up in much hotter climates.

When I was ill and at my worst, I spent many nights on the couch in agony, too exhausted to move and had too many symptoms, our social life became non-existent, as I was never sure how many hours I would be pain free for or when my symptoms would flare up, I will always be grateful to Wayne for his patience and understanding.

After many years of research and education I can now say with certainty that the periods of illness I have had including endometriosis and a Spastic Colon (IBS) are directly related to the diet and lifestyle choices I made and this makes me passionate and drives me to help clients so they don't have to get to the point of not knowing where to turn, not wanting to continuously take medication but feeling that they have to as they are not aware there might be other options. I also understand that not everyone has as great a support network as I had and I am committed to giving my clients 100% support, this does not mean I let them off the hook, I will still challenge them but I am always there for support and building a community of support.

Through my experiences, working with a number of mentors, coaching, lifestyle and mindset changes I am learning to take 100% responsibility for my life and for my choices and because of that I have been able to overcome the periods of illness, and I now truly believe that there is a solution for 95% of all disease. This solution is through diet and lifestyle changes, we not only need to change our diets but we need to change the way we live our lives, what we value in our lives, who supports us and change our beliefs, it takes all of these things to achieve VITALITY.

I will admit is has not been easy and has been a bumpy ride and I am still learning and overcoming challenges, but after many years I have learnt that it is OK and in fact important to ask for help, no-one got to the top on their own and we all need help and support, by having a support system, a mentor and a coach things happen a lot quicker.

If you are a parent, coach, business owner you offer support to others, and often we do this……we tell everyone else about the support they need how we can help them, save them time and money and frustration but how often do we think of asking for help ourselves? Do you have support and accountability?

The first time I was really ill, I was in continuous pain and not sleeping but I was fortunate enough to have a Dr who admitted that there was nothing that could be done from a medical point of view and that I was welcome to try alternative therapies.

I had endometriosis at the time and was in so much pain, I was not sleeping through the night, I was exhausted from the pain and from the lack of sleep and had very low energy levels and a very low mood. I found a fantastic herbalist and managed to reduce my symptoms but around the same time I was diagnosed with spastic colon – where we lived at the time the internet was pretty non-existent, or the page took ½ an hour or more to load by which time I had lost interest and had something better to do – this was a good thing in some ways. We all know how frightening "Dr Google" can be! I had no idea what a spastic colon was and no one to explain it to me so I ignored it in the hope that it might go away. In hindsight the interesting thing is that both of these diagnoses were after I had spent a year travelling in the USA, UK and Europe, eating processed and non-organic foods. They were also treated as two different illnesses but are in fact very closely linked – this is one of the issues we face in Western Medicine in that the body is treated as separate parts and not as a whole.
For example: you have a headache - take a head ache tablet; and/or you have a stomach ache take another tablet;
but no one looks for the root cause and how these are interlinked and if you can treat the root cause, you can solve the problem rather than just putting a "plaster" on by taking medication and hoping it will go away and these medications come with their own

set of problems as one of my mentors says why take something that has more side effects than you have symptoms.

We were very fortunate in Zimbabwe at the time as all of our food was "grass fed" and "organic", we had no packaged foods and everything was made fresh on a daily basis, after several months my spastic colon cleared up – then after several years, a few of them very stressful we moved back to the UK, and a few years later I was diagnosed with Irritable Bowel syndrome aka spastic colon……and once again I was told there was no cure, I would had to be on medication for the rest of my life and this was the only way to go……..so I went on to several medications, one to control the bloating but that caused constipation, so I was on another medication to control the constipation and then yet other medication for stress which as I mentioned turned out to be a very addictive anti-psychotic medication - now it took me some time to figure this all out, one of the turning points was a business seminar I went to and the motivational speaker, Larry Winget's opening words were "shut up, stop whining and get a life" as you can imagine that didn't go down very well with a lot of people but it made me stop and think! We live in a culture where we give our power away to others, we don't take responsibility for our actions and our decision, it is always someone else's fault, where I come from we call it "munya boy". I bought Larry Winget's book ………his message was that we are all in control of our lives and in control of the decisions we make……….the book still sits on my shelf as a reminder to "shut up, stop whining and get a life"

Now I don't think I had ever blamed anyone else for my illness but I had become a "victim" you know the poor me attitude, I'm so sick, I'm on all these medications, I'm not well today, I can't do this, I can't do that because of my symptoms and so my illness was serving me in some way but more about this in Step 1. I had always been interested in health and fitness and then I started taking on board the idea of taking 100% responsibility, now don't get me wrong I admit I got a bit lost along the way and at times went back to being a victim and complaining but I decided to come off all my medication and find a solution to my health problems. I am not in any way suggesting that you do this as it was a personal choice for me, and in some cases stopping medication "cold turkey" can bring about its own set of problems so I always advise working with your health care provider if you decide this may be an option for you.

When I did this I decided there must be another way but I wasn't 100% sure what I needed to do.

I trained as a personal trainer and then discovered although I love exercise and helping others with their fitness and health goals, I was more passionate about nutrition. What you eat, how you eat, your mindset and lifestyle have more of an impact on your health than just the exercise, you have heard the saying "you can't out train a bad diet". I worked as a personal trainer for a while but it was not something that I was truly passionate about and was more of a "job", the more I studied nutrition the more I understood that there was another way to optimal health and Vitality........looking back the worst thing the Dr ever said to me was that here was "no cure", there was nothing I could do except live on medication and live with symptoms, and I now find that one of the most challenging things to deal with, to get client's to the point of having hope and accepting that there are different paths and solutions that they can explore.

Many people are told on a daily basis that they will not heal for anything ranging from IBS and diabetes to many chronic illnesses...........I understand perhaps from my Dr's point of view that the fact there was no solution apart from medication was her belief but I realised it did not have to be mine so I continued on my journey to heal myself without medication, it has taken a large investment (a number of years, a lot of research and a lot of money) and I now work with a coach and mentor and an amazing support group because as I said I learnt along the way that we all need support, you can't change your life overnight but it's easier and quicker to do it with support than on your own. You also need someone outside of your circle who will challenge you to grow, to face and overcome your fears, because if you don't challenge yourself you will not change. As one of my mentors says "if you change the way you look at things, the things you look at change"

When people decide that they are powerless, they also start to become irresponsible. We start to use excuses we blame our genes, our health and then ask "What can you expect from me? I can't do anything about it."

It is because of my journey that I am very passionate about working towards optimal health and vitality, and I truly believe that this is possible through the food we eat, the way we live our lives, our thoughts and beliefs and the success strategies that we implement in our day to day lives, as this is how I healed myself and how I have helped numerous clients overcome their health challenges. All you have to do is take 100% responsibility be open minded, be curious and ask questions.

If you are thinking that a book with the title "If you Believe you can heal yourself you can" is a bit "out there" then thank you for at least getting this far. In our home we call it "the crazy train" but you know what sometimes you have to be on the crazy train to think and believe you can heal yourself and by the way that's a great place to be - so come with me for a ride on the "crazy train" and I promise you rich rewards in health and happiness.

As Steve Jobs very famously said "Here's to the crazy ones, the misfits, the rebels, the troublemakers, the round pegs in the square holes... the ones who see things differently -- they're not fond of rules... You can quote them, disagree with them, glorify or vilify them, but the only thing you can't do is ignore them because they change things... they push the human race forward, and while some may see them as the crazy ones, we see genius, because the ones who are crazy enough to think that they can change the world, are the ones who do".

The information in this book is based on my story and my journey to optimal health and happiness. The information is provided for informational purposes only and is not a substitute for professional medical advice. You should not use the information for diagnosing or treating a medical or health condition. If you have or suspect you have an urgent medical problem, promptly contact your professional healthcare provider. If you choose to, I always advise that you work closely with and under the guidance of a qualified Nutritional Therapist

My hope and intention is that you will read the book with an open mind, explore any of the healing modalities that you think will work for you and to keep this as a reference, as you work to optimal health you can refer back to certain chapters and explore other avenues when you are ready. None of this is rocket science, it is nothing new but at different times we are more open to information, the way it is shared or we are just ready to take on board new information and my hope is that this book starts you on your journey……..

I understand, I have been where you are!

When I started on my journey if anyone had suggested energy healing or spirituality, I probably - in fact I would definitely have scoffed at them saying that it wasn't for me and that it wouldn't work for me.

Religion always raised too many questions for me that could not be answered, I always struggled with religion and had some experiences that made me decide that religion was not for me. BUT I knew there was something bigger out there and when I re-discovered my spirituality, it was something that made sense to me. It has been a long way into my healing journey, but I really feel this is the last piece of the puzzle for me. So I ask you not to disregard anything, always be open minded and ask, there is a lot we have learned but there is a lot that we do not fully understand yet, especially when it comes to mind-body medicine and nutrition, our genes and our microbiome (the world of bacteria living inside us). What you eat, your nutrition is an important part of the puzzle, but your emotions, your thoughts and your lifestyle all have a significant impact on your health.

I have included a number of books at the end that helped me on my journey, they are books that were recommended to me by friends and mentors and have given me a great purpose and understanding and I encourage you to have a look at the list and read the ones that resonate with you.

Having hope and believing that healing is possible is the first step. In my experience if people don't believe that it is possible to heal then they won't even try, they will not be looking for answers, they will have given away their power and won't want to take personal responsibility, so congratulations as you have taken the first step as you wouldn't be reading this book if you didn't believe it was possible.

STEP 1
MIND YOUR MIND: THOUGHTS AND EMOTIONS

Healing is a state of being / a state of knowing. One of the reasons sickness occurs is because of stress, this stress can be physical or emotional and creates and imbalance in the body, it affects our mind, body and spirit. Emotional stress is a result of what you think! 90% of all illness is caused by stress; in fact Bruce Lipton takes this further and says that 95% of all illness is caused by stress. Stress creates an imbalance in the body leading to symptoms which if we ignore lead to a loss of health.

If your thoughts are negative you will always focus on the negative, finding problems instead of looking for solutions. Remember that all things are possible so don't put limitations on yourself – the only hindrance to healing is the belief that there is a hindrance to healing.

Did you know your reality as you know it is an illusion?

What you believe and perceive you will create – "As a man thinks so is he" this will be your experience whether it is good or bad. Earl Nightingale said *"You become what you think of most of the time"*. It may not be the truth but it will be you reality. I see this all the time where people say they are sick and tired, they use handles on forums such as "always in pain"; "sickandtired"; "inagony" – now I am not saying that this is not true, I have been there, and all of these could of applied to me and I very well may of registered on a forum using one of these "handles" but I just ask you to think about this – say "I am sad" out loud 5 times and then say "I am happy" out loud 5 times, just trust me and try this out and see how you feel, so now do you understand why what you say to yourself matters?

The most important decision you will ever make if whether or not we believe this universe is friendly or hostile – Albert Einstein

I know that if you have been labelled with an illness such as IBS, Chronic Fatigue, Adrenal Fatigue often you will be told this is "all in your head". I was told this on a number of occasions and I know this is very frustrating. When someone has an external physical injury people get it, but when your "injuries" are internal no-one can see them and people don't often understand how much pain you can be in. I also know that most people who are ill in any way find it very frustrating to be told that positive thinking will get them through any illness, now I am in no way suggesting that it is just in your head and that only positive thinking will get you well but stay with me a moment, I did mention being open minded............

Did you know that a belief is just a thought that you think over and over and over again? It is not necessarily true; it is just something that is formed via repetition and we can simply change our beliefs, isn't that exciting? Our brains are very efficient super-computers and they assess and filter information, and then either accept or reject this information. Once the information is accepted it becomes a belief and then once it becomes a belief it is stored the same way a computer stores a programme. Did you ever believe something as a child and then grew up to find it wasn't true. We were told things like if you pulled a funny face and the wind changed your face would stay that way, if you swallowed the pips from fruit, fruit trees would grow out of your ears...... now I know these are funny beliefs and possibly things you may question and they are meant to stop you doing these things as kids, but the point is that we were told these things repeatedly by people who were older than us, people we saw as being in a position of authority who we thought knew better than us and we did not have anything to compare this to, so we believed them for a while. Most of us are given beliefs by our parents that we never question, beliefs about relationships, health, ageing, money, careers etc that we never question and yet they have no basis in truth. It is not that our parents lied to us, but these are beliefs that they were probably given by their parents and they passed them on thinking they would protect us. Think for example, if you were told you would catch a cold if you went to bed with wet hair, a cold is a virus and in reality has very little to do with wet hair. If you are unhealthy and your immune system is low then yes you are more susceptible to catching the cold but more on that in Step 2.

The thoughts you have about your life, your world, become your reality - physical changes happen due to what is happening in your mind – I am not saying that you can sit back and just think about it and not take action, but your thoughts and your beliefs create the environment to enable you to take inspired action to achieve your dreams.

For example: if you keep telling yourself that you are sick and tired, you will always be sick and tired. I challenge you to try this for one week, if someone asks how you are say I am really well thank you, even if you don't feel that well say it and just see how it makes you feel. I am not saying that your symptoms will disappear but you will feel better and the better you feel the more inspired you will be to take the action you need to take to improve your health and start to feel better.

Take a close look at the beliefs you hold in all areas of your life, things like:
- you have to work hard to get anywhere;
- Dr's are always right;
- rich people aren't happy;
- money is evil;
- we get sicker as we get older.

When I sat down and went through all the things I believed, and then questioned them I was amazed at how many beliefs I had that were not serving me, when I really questioned and explored these beliefs I was able to let them go and felt a sense of relief and freedom that I had not had before. I did this in all areas of my life my Health, Family, Career, Finances, Relationships, Personal Growth and Spirituality.

I will share some of the beliefs I had as these may help you and they are the things that changed my health, I start with beliefs and mindset as without these things you can change the way you eat, you can change the way you move but I truly believe that until you change the way you think and change the way you feel you will never truly achieve optimal health, I changed all of these things but it was not until I started to change my beliefs, work on my mindset, meditation and spirituality that things really began to change.

The beliefs I had were:

Dr's know best – my belief now is that I am the only person who truly 100% cares about my health and I will do more to make myself well than anyone else ever will.

The Dr is responsible for my health – crazy right, why give your power away. I am 100% responsible for my health. The minute we start to blame and complain we give our power away to someone else. As soon as you take 100% responsibility you can take action and do something about your health.

You get sicker and as you get older – not true, our bodies genetically can live to 120, it is the food we eat and the way we live our lives that make us sick.

I believed because I was treated that way that all my symptoms were individual – again not true – everything in your body is interlinked. You are only as strong as your weakest system, if your digestion is not working and you are not getting the nutrients you need everything else will start to break down and you end up with aches and pains and ill health. I explore this in more detail in **Step 2.**

You are ill, there is nothing you can do and you cannot heal – again not true, I was not born ill, I got ill overtime due to my diet and lifestyle choices and by changing those I got healthy and removed my symptoms.

I like to get people to take action, another lesson I learned along the way – you can read and read and read, learn everything there is to know but unless you take action nothing will ever change. So throughout the book you will find downloads and areas where you can take action, please use these tools, I didn't make them up just for fun. They are the tools and strategies that help my clients, I may say this over and over again but if you just change the way you eat and you can, this is simple and you will see results. But it is not until you do what I call the "other stuff" that things will truly change.

So here we go:

TAKE ACTION:
1. Write down at least 5 beliefs that you have right now. If you have more than 5 keep you can do this in stages, the more you can work on and change the better but I don't want this to be overwhelming so lets' start with five. As you write them down they may seem very solid or they may start to seem slightly ridiculous when you say them out loud and write them down, that's OK it happens, just write them down.
2. Read each belief out loud and ask yourself these questions: Is this really true? How do I know it is true? Is this belief serving me? Do I have proof that this is true? If not, let it go. Feel the sense of relief and the opening for you to form a new belief, a healthier belief that serves you?
3. Remember beliefs are your choice, are they serving you? Are they stopping you form achieving your goals or dreams? You make your beliefs true by the thoughts you keep thinking over and over and over again. A great thing to do is constantly question these beliefs and learn to think new and different thoughts and create new beliefs.
4. We do not need to change beliefs that serve us, for example if you believe you can heal yourself you can, this is a positive belief, it give you the power and responsibility and will serve you when you are ill, if you believe that money is good, this is a great belief to have money is good it enables you to live the life you want, enables you go on holiday to relax and recharge and enables you to give back and help others when you have more money.

I know that you may have some beliefs that are not serving you and don't seem as easy to change and this is where we use techniques such as Emotional Freedom Technique and my personal favourite Theta Healing® to change these to make sure they are serving us positively rather than negatively.

I never understood the saying "where ever you go there you are", have you heard that saying and do you find it confusing or was it just me? Another example, I did understand "the grass is always greener on the other side" if you are not happy and healthy you can look at moving home, jobs, countries as I thought about doing but make the move and the grass will still be greener "on the other side" from where ever you are because you haven't changed – you still have the same thoughts, the same beliefs and the same attitude. You do not become healthier or happier just by moving you are the same person with the same issues (unless you have dealt with them) so very basically happy and healthy are inside / internal things they are not external.

So however happy and healthy you are depends on how you treat yourself, how you speak to yourself (the voice in your head), when, how and what you eat, how you sleep, move and think and unless you change those "wherever you go there you are"

We now live in an environment almost unrecognisable from the environment we evolved in. There is a lot of information and misinformation in the public domain about environmental factors that affect health and how well our body can/cannot deal with them. It can be hard to understand what is 'myth' and what is important to focus on and the extent to which testing and nutrition and lifestyle interventions can actually make a difference. Our lives and health depend on taking control of our thoughts (our minds), which form our beliefs and affect the choices we make, affects our mood and how we live our daily lives.

You can change how you feel by changing the negative moods and beliefs that hold us back or keep us being a "victim" of our illness. We need to be aware of our stories as we give them power and believe they are real and we can end up suffering - when we see that they are just thoughts we allow ourselves to be free to respond and behave differently and create a new story

I have used a number of techniques over the years from when I first discovered Emotional Freedom Technique (EFT), Meditation in various forms from Guided Meditations to Transcendental

Meditation, using a Gratitude Journal and to early this year I was led to qualify as a *Theta Healer®*.

Emotional Freedom Technique, or EFT (often known as Tapping or EFT Tapping), is a universal healing tool that can be used for physical and emotional issues, it is effective for physical issues, and chronic pain. It is now well know that any kind of stress emotional and physical stress can slow down the natural healing potential of the human body, so by removing the stress we can speed up the healing process.

EFT can be used directly for relief from physical symptoms without going into any emotional factors but for powerful and longer lasting relief identifying and targeting the emotional issues is necessary. EFT borrows from the Chinese meridian system and combines the physical benefits of acupuncture with the cognitive benefits of conventional therapy for faster results.

I personally don't use EFT as much now as I find Theta Healing far more effective, but I do find this a simple and easy tool for most people to use and to get instant relief from stress. You can do this anytime, anywhere and it is quick and can be very simple. Here is a link to a basic youtube video I created click here or follow the link : http://bit.ly/1RcwaU2 (This is for information purposes only and I always recommend you work with a qualified EFT practitioner, I have since qualified as a Positive EFT Facilitator). My initial introduction to EFT was via the internet through Gary Craig's website www.emofree.com and then through webinars and the online Tapping Summit with Nick and Jessica Ortner, their website is www.thetappingsolution.com. I went on to train as a Positive EFT facilitator as I found the process very powerful and wanted to be able to use this with my clients. The thing that I do like most about EFT is that once you know the tapping points you can use this anywhere anytime, one of the things I am passionate about is to empower people to have tools that they can use on their own and use for the rest of their lives.

You can get the basic information and tapping points here : http://www.emofree.com/eft-tutorial/tapping-basics/how-to-do-eft.html.

Some additional practical advice on EFT that worked for me – keep it simple and don't get caught up with worrying about the correct words, whatever words have an attachment for you or even just feeling the emotions will give you some relief. If you do not feel that you are able to work on this on your own or you are dealing with severe pain or emotional issues, I would encourage you to seek out an EFT practitioner to work with – please see the reference section at the end of the book for contact details of the AAMET, the professional body of EFT practitioners and you can find the right practitioner for you. It is possible to do this over skype as well as in person and my personal advice would be to have a conversation or ensure you have a recommendation of someone to work with and to ensure that you comfortable working with the EFT practitioner you have chosen.

Meditation
Meditation is another effective tool for stress relief, for gratitude and for overall wellness. I am sure you have heard the saying if you have 20 minutes meditate if you have no time, meditate for an hour.

I know what you are thinking, that to meditate you have to sit in total silence and chant "om", but let me explain some different ways to meditate as this is something I struggled with for a long time before I found a strategy that worked for me. I thought that you had to sit in total silence with no thoughts and just relax – well let me just take a load off your mind – that is never going to happen. I tried for months and every time I sat down to meditate I thought of all the chores I had to do and just got more stressed and tense and gave up thinking I could not meditate, have you had this experience?

Meditation is this simple……. Sit in a comfortable position and focus on your breathing – you can then expand this and make sure you are taking deep breaths that reach your abdomen rather than the shallow breathing we all tend to do that only reaches our chest, some other techniques are to breathe in for a count of five and then breathe out for a count of seven. You can sit and focus on a lit candle or a picture or a particular word – these are all methods of meditation, they bring you into the present moment and allow you to focus on something other than your thoughts, when your thoughts drift in let them go and re-focus on the breathing, candle etc

Guided Meditation
My personal advice is to start with guided meditations, a word of caution you do need to find someone who you find relaxing to listen to as it is really hard to meditate and relax if you are listening to some with a voice that you find annoying or irritating. I personally started with the Deepak Chopra free 21 day meditations. For me it was a great way to start and I always refer my 1-1 clients to these meditations as a starting point.

I have included a Guided Mediation for you in the downloads section.

Transcendental Meditation
I then went on to learn Transcendental Meditation and I actually physically and scientifically tested the effects of the meditation with a stress test – I was hooked up to a monitor and had my heart rate tested, my results were pretty poor showing that I was incredibly stressed. I then attended a 2 day Transcendental Meditation course and continued to meditate and after just one week I had the same test done again and my results were completely reversed.

Many people report that the TM technique has a transforming effect, there have been major benefits reported from reducing chronic stress and anxiety, insomnia, hypertension, and other stress-related disorders.

There are over 380 published, peer-reviewed research studies on the TM technique have documented its effectiveness for stress-related conditions, brain function, and more. See the resources section at the end for more information.

Theta Healing ®Meditation

Our brain is made of billions of brain cells, neurons. These neurons use electricity to communicate with each other and produce an enormous amount of electrical activity in the brain, this is called a brainwave pattern as it has a wave like pattern. We have different types of brainwaves and these are known as:

Beta: this is our normal state when we are consciously awake and alert, the frequency ranges from 14 – 30Hz
Alpha: This frequency is around 9 – 13hz and when we are in Alpha we are in a state of physical and mental relaxation – this is the state we achieve for most meditative states
Theta: 4-Hz, Theta is a state of very deep relaxation; this is used in hypnosis and REM sleep. People meditate for consecutively for hours to achieve this state. Theta is considered to be our subconscious – it is believe that when we are in Theta we act below the level of the conscious mind.
Delta: 1 -3 Hz – unconscious deep sleep.

During Theta meditation our brainwaves are at a very low frequency between 4 – 8 hz, this is very close to Delta brain waves which are the lowest frequency brain waves that you can achieve. When you are in theta meditation you are in an extremely relaxed state.

Through Transcendental Meditation or Theta Mediation we are able to actually affect our cortisol levels, in some studies cortisol is reduced by as much as 47% and there is an increase in DHEA which is a precursor to every hormone in your body (1)

"By quieting the mind, which then quiets the body, and the less turbulent the body is, the more the self-repair healing mechanisms get amplified. In fact, scientists have shown that the better your DNA, your genetic machinery is at healing itself, the longer you live. That's how meditation lowers biological age." Deepak Chopra

The Physical Benefits of Meditation

During mediation our physiology undergoes a change and every cell in the body is filled with more energy, as the energy (life force) in the body increases this results in feelings of joy, peace and enthusiasm

On a purely physical level, meditation
- Lowers high blood pressure
- Lowers the levels of blood lactate - when oxygen delivery is insufficient blood lactate rises. Reducing the level can reduce anxiety attacks
- Decreases tension related pain : headaches, ulcers, insomnia, muscle and joint issues
- Increases serotonin production which improves mood and behaviour
- Improves the immune system

With regular practice of meditation
- Anxiety decreases
- Joy and happiness increases
- Creativity increases
- Intuition develops
- Emotional stability improves
- Problems seem smaller
- Clarity and peace of mind
- More focus
- Sharpens the mind
- Expanded consciousness
- Emotional steadiness and harmony

Meditation helps to make us aware that our inner attitude determines our happiness.

My life changed significantly when I began to meditate, as you learn more about yourself, you start discovering more about yourself. Meditation is like a seed, you need to cultivate the seed with love, the more you cultivate is, the more it blooms.

Getting the benefits:
In order to get the benefits of mediation, regular practice is necessary. It only needs to take a few minutes every day. Put it in your dairy as an appointment with yourself; try it for at least 7 days, once it is part of your daily routine it will become the best part of your day!

I encourage you to pause, reflect and enjoy a few minutes of mediation each day, this can be as little as 5 to 10 minutes. Often it is the simple things in life that make the most significant changes and meditation is one of those simple things that can have a profound difference in your life.

No excuses! Download your free mediation now and try one, there are 3 to choose from: Guided Mediation, Theta Meditation or the Quick Relaxation Track

Get Your Downloads - Click Here for Kindle readers or follow the Link : http://bit.ly/1IesejE

Gratitude
"Gratitude, thankfulness, gratefulness, or appreciation is a feeling or attitude in acknowledgment of a benefit that one has received or will receive" from Wikipedia, the free encyclopaedia.

Having a Gratitude Journal is something I have done for a number of years, I do this my clients and I encourage everyone to start a Gratitude Journal. There are specific Gratitude Journals you can buy, but you can start with a notepad: everyday write down at least three things you are grateful for and then start to notice the changes in your life. The more things you are grateful for the more things you will have to be grateful for, I promise this works, another of those simple tools that has profound effects.

A Gratitude Journal encourages you to look for the good in your life and helps you to focus on the positive rather than the negative. When I first started, some days all I wrote down were that I was grateful my kettle worked, I was grateful to have a roof over my head – we often tend to forget about the little things and life gets out of perspective.

Did you know that:
"If you have food in your fridge, clothes on your back, a roof over your head and a place to sleep you are richer than 75% of the world.

If you have money in the bank, your wallet, and some spare change you are among the top 8% of the worlds wealthy.

If you woke up this morning with more health than illness you are more blessed than the million people who will not survive this week.

If you can read this message you are more fortunate than 3 billion people in the world who cannot read it at all."

Gratitude is about expressing thanks and appreciation for what we already have, rather than focusing on what we want or don't have. Studies show that by cultivating and attitude of gratitude we can increase our well-being and happiness; it is associated with increased energy and optimism.

We live in a society where people are mostly comparing and despairing, we look at what we have in comparison to others and despair that we may not have what they have or what they "appear to have. People live their best lives on social media platforms and we end up comparing our worst days with someone else's best days and feel like we fall short. But you have no idea of what that person is really going through, how happy they really are, what their relationships are like, about the things that truly matter in life.

TAKE ACTION

Gratitude : Try one of these way of expressing your Gratitude every day
- Daily Gratitude Journal: 3 – 5 things you are grateful for
- Daily 5 minute journal: including things you are grateful for. People, situations, experiences etc
- Gratitude Walk – focus on what you are grateful for

Pick one method and practice this daily – like meditation to see the benefits you need to do this on a daily basis

Get Your Downloads - Click Here for Kindle readers or follow the Link : http://bit.ly/1IesejE

Theta Healing®
Theta Healing is by far the best and quickest method for identifying and releasing negative thoughts and beliefs that I have found, it has a profound effect on my life and on my client's in the short time I have been using it.

I have included some information below as it is best explained by Vianna Stibal , the creator of The ThetaHealing® technique, which was created in 1995 during her own personal journey back to health :

Theta Healing® works on *all levels of your being*: emotional, physical, mental and spiritual, by clearing the blocks and obstacles that are preventing you from achieving your fullest potential in your life. Theta Healing® is an extremely profound healing treatment yet *very gentle*. The healing actually comes from the infinite source of divine energy, the Creator.

I am a certified Theta Healing® practitioner; and although I have been working with Theta Healing for a relatively short time, since March 2015 it is my one of my favourite techniques to use with clients. I love empowering clients to discover their own infinite inner resources to grow and live their lives in health and happiness.

I discovered Theta Healing® as part of my own spiritual journey. My journey to optimal health and happiness has led me to many therapeutic approaches and these have now become the basis for what works so successfully with my clients, Theta Healing® has changed my life completely, and I now use this in a number of ways with my clients and it always give my clients calm and inner peace instantly.

Downloads: If you would like to have these downloads then just say "YES" take a deep breath and be open to receiving:

Would you like to know what it feels like, how to and that you do love yourself, that you know you are loved, that you are allowed to sense know and feel deep love for yourself and send this love out to others constantly. That you know what it feels like and how to honor yourself by going within and understanding the immense beauty there - If you want this say yes and be open to receive.

Would you like to know that you allow beauty to flow through you constantly inspiring yourself and others to health, prosperity and abundance?

Would you like to know what it feels like, how to and that you do allow energy to love and nourish you to wholeness, health and prosperity? - If you want this say yes and be open to receive

Would you like to know what it feels, like, how to and that you do have creators wisdom, courage, honesty and self love to look deep within and see what is there? To have creators knowledge that I you are allowed to, that you know how to, you know what it feels like and I that you can reprogram the beliefs that prevent you from effectively healing myself and my life - If you want this say yes and be open to receive

Close your eyes, take a deep breath and relax and allow the downloads

Support

Implementing changes can be challenging. The problem and the solution are the same for any challenge or change we need to make, whether this is work related, diet related etc etc. When I try to make changes I am reminded about the whole idea of trying to change too many things at once, becoming overwhelmed and failing to implement the changes, and one of the major reasons we fail to implement changes is due to lack of support and accountability. Often we may either know what to do or we have an idea of what needs to be done, but we still don't do it because we will do it *"tomorrow"* and you all know what tomorrow never comes.

I like to change things overnight - but in some cases this doesn't work in creating long term success, we can get overwhelmed and 9 times out of 10 give up as it becomes too difficult or you start failing on changing one things and think "oh well it doesn't matter, if I can't get that one thing right why bother with the rest" - does this sound familiar?

So why do we struggle?

Most of us try to do this alone, if you end up faltering because of one slip up, there is no one to support you and cheer you on and then you may end failing as we tell ourselves, that it is too hard and talk ourselves out of it, we convince ourselves that it was never going to work so we can justify our actions and feel better about it - I know you are all smiling it's human nature we have all done this possibly many, many times over. I know I have!

So how can you make changes successfully?
Find your "cheerleaders"

I will give you a recent example, I was struggling on my own, trying to make some changes I needed to make in my business, now although this may seem different from making diet and lifestyle changes the principles are the same – support, accountability and encouragement. I needed to find my cheerleaders, so I signed up and paid for a four day course that helped me define the changes I needed to make, I also have ongoing support and in a week I made the changes that I had been needing to make for months. Of course I tell my clients this all the time........ you need support, find a support network, but sometimes it is challenging to ask for help and we always think we can just do it on our own, I know I was guilty of that, you know those beliefs I was talking about in Step 1, I believed that to be successful I had to achieve everything on my own, that people would judge me if I asked for help that I would be seen as weak, I know you may find this hard to believe, saying them out load they sound silly, but I truly believed this. These beliefs were not serving me and now sound ridiculous when I write them or say them out loud, and now whenever I need help or support I find the people I need to make.

I now call these people **cheerleaders**: (*warning: these may or may not be the people closest to you.......). These are the people who will support you through your lifestyle changes, the ones who will talk you out of having that extra helping by reminding you of your goal or will offer to share a piece of cake with you, if you really, really want it. Do you find that in most instances everyone says "one biscuit wouldn't hurt" or "one cup of coffee won't make any difference" - these people bless them are not your cheerleaders. Most often they are the people who are the closest to us and it is not that they want us to fail, but if we are successful at making changes it means they may have to look at their habits and lifestyle and make changes and that may be uncomfortable for them.

In my personal experience and the experience with my clients I find the best ways to do this is through a group that will offer you support, you don't want to be the one who fails to implement the changes, and no-one else in the group wants you to fail and this gives you the motivation to succeed and implement long term changes. I am the "cheerleader" to all my clients and when they are part of my group programmes, they become cheerleaders for each other. Mostly, they know they can do it, but sometimes they just need the support to know that someone else knows they can do it too.

TAKE ACTION

You don't have to do all of these things but working on your mindset is one of the most important things you can do. So I would encourage you to work on your mindset every day.

Choose one type of meditation; find the one that works best for you. Start your gratitude journal and find your cheerleaders and I promise you, you will see significant changes in your life. Don't force these changes just observe and notice what changes take place in your life.

STEP 2
NOURISH YOUR BODY AND MIND: NUTRITION

Are you one of those people who is not totally convinced that what you put in your body directly affects how you feel but you have to have a cup of coffee to get you going?

Here is a very simple example:

Pre coffee: you are sleepy
Post-coffee: you are wide awake
Lesson: what you put in your body has a direct and enormous impact on how you feel

And P.S. NO this is not a go-ahead to drink coffee, I just want you to connect the dots that what you put in your body directly affects the way you feel. We will explore the issues with coffee the further we get into this step.

The way you eat, the way you think and the choices you make can influence your life by 30-50 years. Motivation is what gets you started and habits and results keep you going

There are millions of books available on what to eat, when to eat, how to eat, clean eating, raw eating, paleo diets, vegan, vegetarian, you may be disappointed but I am not going to tell you which diet is best for you but I will give you some basic rules to follow so you can work out what the best way for you to eat is. I will let you know the foods to avoid and why you should avoid them and I have included a meal plan and recipes in the resource section for you to try.

My intention is that you understand why we recommend avoiding the foods we do, mainly because they cause issues with your gut, affecting your digestion and absorption of nutrients, this leads to inflammation and auto-immune reactions and to a loss of health. Working alongside mindfulness, gratitude, the right foods, movement, the right amount of sleep and reducing stress we can start working on healing the gut for optimal health.

The best piece of advice I can give you is listen to your body, if you are eating something that is supposed to be healthy, but it is adding to your symptoms then guess what it is not healthy for you, keeping a food and mood journal may be seem boring and tedious but unless you are already listening to your body, and if you are then congratulations! But if you are not, then this is one of the best ways you can learn to connect the dots and start to listen to your body. When I was ill I was eating foods that are healthy, but because my digestion was compromised these foods were hard to digest and added to my symptoms, however, once I healed my gut I was able to re-introduce these foods without any problems.

Most of the clients I work with are misled about what is healthy and what is not-healthy, every time you eat you have the option of reducing inflammation in the body or increasing it, for example cereal and milk first thing in the morning will add to your inflammation, but if you eat a good protein rich breakfast, organic eggs and bacon, wild salmon and eggs, a green protein smoothie then you are reducing the inflammation in the body, balancing your blood sugars and giving your body the fuel it needs. Once you understand which foods may be best for you and which foods may not be then you can't use the excuse you didn't know – yes you can still decide to go ahead and eat those foods anyway knowing the damage they are causing to your body but then that is your choice, you decide. You always have a choice but you may think twice and PS: yes I do hope to change the way you eat.

Too many people are eating their way into illness, it can take up to 14 years for the full effects of an autoimmune condition to manifest, you will have signs and symptoms along the way but mostly we ignore those until we are really ill and once you suffer from one autoimmune condition you are likely to suffer from at least 2 or 3 others.

A person may have more than one autoimmune disorder at the same time. Common autoimmune disorders include:

- Addison's disease – affects the adrenal glands
- Celiac disease - (gluten allergy)
- Dermatomyositis – skin inflammation and rash
- Graves' disease – overactive thyroid
- Hashimoto's thyroiditis – reduced thyroid function
- Multiple sclerosis
- Pernicious anaemia
- Reactive arthritis
- Rheumatoid arthritis
- Sjogren syndrome
- Systemic lupus erythematosus
- Type I diabetes

Even if you do not have an auto-immune condition, if you are suffering from any symptoms such as joint aches and pains, headaches, PMT or PMS, gas, bloating, indigestion, acid reflux these are all signs that something is not right, it is your body's way of signalling to you that something needs to change.

One thing I would like to make clear is that none of these symptoms are normal, they may be common but they are not normal.

Our bodies are designed to be well – like a car, if you give your body the right fuel it will run optimally, but start to change anything, the quality of the fuel, oil and water and just like a car your body will start breaking down more and more often.

Be grateful for your symptoms, they are signs from your body to change the way you eat, they are letting you know that the body is out of balance. I know you have probably heard this many times before but if you keep doing what you have been doing, you will get what you have already got, you all know Albert Einstein's definition of Insanity: "doing the same thing over and over again and expecting different results."

I see this so often with my clients they think they can just make a few changes and it will all work out but you need to commit 100% - they only way you will get different results is if you change what got you to this point and this includes your diet, your lifestyle, the way you think and how you manage your stress.

The body has an incredible capacity to heal but if it keeps breaking down, if the wear and tear is more than the repair, for example if you are not eating a nutrient dense diet, you are stressed and not sleeping very well, then the body is breaking down but it is not getting enough nutrients or time to repair, as most of our repair and regeneration is done at night when we sleep, so if our sleep is compromised the body's ability to heal will also be compromised.

If you want to achieve optimal health and vitality then you most likely will need to change what you eat on a daily basis. I hope to be able to help you make a more informed choice rather than just do what you have been lead to believe or always been told to do. For instance most of us are brought up having sugary cereal and milk for breakfast – this is the worst possible way to start the day as you are being overloaded by sugar from the cereal and the milk, creating a blood sugar imbalance and inflammation is being created from the wheat in the cereal and from the lactose or casein in the milk, never mind the toxins and additives that are put in most of our foods these days, and we wonder why most children can't concentrate at school or why most people can't concentrate at work, why you are craving caffeine and food by 10am and feeling tired and suffering from headaches etc.

When it comes to what we eat (I am referring to protein, carbs and fats), how often we eat, we are all individual and there is no one size fits all, so it is about taking the basics and making them work for you. For example, I am at my best when I get my carbohydrates from vegetables, I have loads of energy and feel fabulous, but I have clients who have to have carbohydrates at every single meal. The best meal for you will be one that leaves you full of energy, with no cravings and no symptoms such as feeling uncomfortable or having gas, bloating or indigestion. If you have any of these symptoms after you eat, then something you are eating is not the best choice for you.

The first step in working towards optimal health is to remove all toxic and allergenic foods, I have included a list of the top 7 most inflammatory foods and why these are inflammatory to the body to help you understand the effects they have on the body and on our health.

The 7 most common Inflammatory Foods

#1
Wheat and all types of gluten containing flour - rye, spelt, gram, wheat germ, brown, white or whole meal

This is partly due to the fact that we now eat this in large quantities – it is not only found in bread, pasta, biscuits, pastries but in many tinned foods and sauces as it is used a bulking agent - the proteins in wheat can irritate the GI Tract and the intestinal wall. I know you probably keep hearing about gluten over and over again and you may be wondering why there is such a big fuss about gluten, or you may think that it is not a problem unless you suffer from Celiac disease but Dr Fasano discovered that gluten directly impacts the intestinal lining through zonulin production. Zonulin is a protein that directly causes leaky gut, if you have any symptoms from bloating and gas to joint pain - you could possibly have a leaky gut - gluten also contributes to the formation of antibodies, which can cause the secretion of inflammatory chemicals leading to tissue damage and these antibodies can cross react with the tissues of the body causing autoimmune disease.

The wheat that we eat today is not the same wheat as our great-grandparents ate. Since the 1950's our wheat has been modified and genetically engineered to produce higher yields and it now contains a lot more gluten, this combined with the fact that it is so prevalent in our diets adds to the problem.

#2
Dairy Products
Dairy is another problematic food for some people. Lactose intolerance is a common source of digestive issues but it is only one of the many compounds in milk that can cause problems. The main protein is called casein (whey) and this can cause as many issues as lactose intolerance, it also has a cross reaction with other protein, such as the proteins from gluten. An elimination diet is the best way to determine your sensitivity, it is found in almost all

dairy products and in other products such as milk chocolate, sauces, seasonings, protein powders, non-dairy creamers and many processed foods.

#3
Caffeine

Although coffee is full of antioxidants, vitamins, minerals, amino acids, plant-compounds, fats, and carbs, in small amounts, coffee can be beneficial for most healthy individuals BUT the main downside to coffee is that it's highly acidic, and this acidity can have possible repercussions on the gut. It is also a heavily sprayed crop so contains many chemicals that are transferred to the final product that you drink

Drinking coffee regularly and especially in the morning on an empty stomach, reduces the amount of stomach acid available for digestion later on. H. pylori bacteria, which is the main bacteria responsible for ulcers, prefers highly acidic environments and when you combine this with the way coffee weakens the protective barrier of the stomach the risk of leaky gut, damage and ulcers increases.

Caffeine also blocks the messages sent by the body to say you are tired it does not replace rest or energy replenishment

#4
Nightshades

Due to various compounds such as alkaloids in these foods can cause issues for people with compromised digestion. Common nightshades include white potatoes, eggplant, tomatoes and peppers as well as spices made from peppers.

They do not cause issues for most people but if your gut is compromised and immune system is weakened it is a good idea to avoid these until you have started to heal your gut. Alkaloids can increase your immune response and this something you want to avoid when trying to heal your gut.

Most of the evidence to avoid nightshades is anecdotal, in other words it comes from results from clients and patients who have had relief from avoiding nightshades, my theory is always if in doubt don't and doing a elimination diet and re-testing these foods is recommended.

#5
Processed foods
Due to various artificial additives and chemicals that add to our toxic load and can add harm the mucosal lining leading to leaky gut.

Food Manufacturers often make foods in a laboratory and not in a kitchen. They make them as rewarding as possible which leads to us over consuming the foods because they "taste nice", we are led to eat with our taste buds. They need to add chemicals and additives to these foods to make then edible but they are not concerned about the impact of these faux foods our health. Processed foods are often high in sugar, these can be on the label as anything from sugar to High Fructose Corn Syrup and we know that sugar causes inflammation. Processed foods also contain high amounts of refined carbohydrates which lead to rapid sugar spikes in the body and we are back to square one with inflammation in the body. Most processed foods are also low in nutrients, they may contain synthetic nutrients but the body does not recognise these and they are no substitute for real nutrients from real food.

When we talk about processed foods we are talking about packaged and frozen foods that you can buy in the supermarket, they come in a box, a packet or a can. We are not talking about basic processing for instance turning an apple into a homemade apple sauce at home.

#6
Soy

Soy is in many processed foods, and contains proteins that can cause sensitivities. Even if you don't think you eat soy once you start reading food labels you may be surprised to find out where soy is getting into your diet. The main types of soy to avoid are edamame, tofu, tempeh, soy milk, soy protein and soy imitation meats: check your food labels for any form of soy protein it can be added to anything from protein powders to fillers for meat patties and sausages.

There is a lot of controversy over soy, I would always avoid any soy products that are from a GMO (Genetically-modified) and non-fermented source. I have had colleagues who have had success using fermented, organic and non-GMO soy with clients, but as always my advice with everything is to test it and see if it something you can tolerate or not but always ensure you are using the highest quality organic NON-GMO and fermented forms of soy.

#7
Sugar and artificial sweeteners

Artificial sweeteners and artificial preservatives can also be highly irritating to the gut – things to include in this list are sugar alternatives such as xyilitol as sugar alcohols can cause GI distress. Sugar is a highly inflammatory food whether you have gut issues or not.

A word of caution: Please remember that although these are the most common and the top 7 allergenic and inflammatory foods (they irritate the gut and create and inflammatory response in the body), you may find that other foods cause a reaction. These other foods can be HEALTHY foods; they may just not be healthy for you right now. Before many of my clients start working with me, they feel that they are reacting to everything and my advice would be to always complete a food diary for 4 – 7 days, do an elimination diet, and listen to your body to be able to determine your trigger foods. There is no need to eliminate foods that are not your triggers.

As an example one of my clients was intolerant to ginger, now ginger is fantastic anti-inflammatory and something I consider a must in most people's diets but for this one client everything they ate with ginger caused a reaction, but once they were able to determine it was just the ginger and could remove this, many symptoms cleared up and then once they had followed a gut healing plan they were actually able to reintroduce and tolerate ginger, so it was just an issue with the gut that needed to be solved.

If you are suffering from any symptoms, joint pain, headaches, digestive disorders, allergies etc all of these are related to an imbalance in the body related to issues with gut health, toxicity and acidity in the body and emotional wellbeing. The only way to ease and control your symptoms, increase your energy levels and take back control of your life is through changing your diet, taking the right supplements for you, dealing with any emotional issues and changing your lifestyle and your beliefs around your health.

I highly recommend that you try one of the following:
- An elimination diet: this is where you eliminate all allergenic foods for a minimum of 4 weeks up to 12 weeks and then slowly on a rotational basis re-introduce these foods back into your diet to identify which foods are causing your symptoms.
- 7 or 14 or 28 day detox and cleanse : this would consist of removing allergenic foods, processed and refined foods and increasing your intake of alkalising vegetables, juices and smoothies mainly with green, alkalising vegetables and detoxifying herbs and including specific natural and herbal cleanse capsules
- The FODMAP diet: if you were told to try a high fibre diet and this did not work or made your symptoms worse and if you feel the elimination diet is not for you, then try the FODMAP diet. The term FODMAPs was coined by two Australian researchers Susan J. Shepherd and Peter R. Gibson; they discovered that a low FODMAP diet many patients. A low FODMAP diet avoids foods containing certain sugars and fibres. Remember this is

not a prescription and every food you try has to be done by trial and error to see what works for you. You will also need to ensure that you supplement with a good quality multi-strain probiotic as by eliminating FODMAPs you will be reducing your intake of natural pre and pro biotics.

I would always recommend working under the guidance of a qualified nutritional therapist when attempting any of the diets mentioned above.

Hippocrates who is considered the father of Western Medicine stated that all disease begins in the Gut and Samuel Thomson a herbalist and botanist thought of the stomach as the place where the flow of life and energy began and he believed that by clearing the stomach you could automatically alleviate disease.

Working on healing the digestion is not something new, and as we face more and more illness and disease we are returning to the old ways of healing our body and incorporating them with new information along with healing the body, mind and spirit together instead of as separate entities.

Let's talk about digestion for a bit so you can get a basic picture of how important this is to your overall health. When we are stressed our body is in "flight or fight" and preparing to fight or run away from the perceived danger (this is either emotional or physical, the body cannot determine if it is real or imagined, physical or emotional and reacts in the same way) – in very basic terms we have "fight/flight" mode or "rest/digest" mode and when we are in one we cannot be in the other and fight/flight mode will always take precedence as this is for our basic survival.

To start healing our digestion we need to look at liver health and rebalancing the gut. When the liver is healthy, intestinal inflammation is reduced, gut bacteria is balanced and motility is improved the gut can start to repair and heal

These are the steps I follow with my clients:

1. Remove and Revitalise: Removing inflammatory foods and starting to revitalise the digestive system with the right foods so it can begin to heal. Working on emotional issues and removing stress both emotional and physical.
2. Replace and Detox: Increasing fibre in the diet, this has to be done slowly as most of us are not eating enough fibre and cannot tolerate a sudden increase in fibre. Fibre is also one of the best ways we have of helping our body to rid itself of toxins, we also need to know how and where to remove toxins from our personal environment
3. Repopulate and Energise: Replacing the good bacteria, digestive enzymes and ensuring good levels of stomach acid and increasing energy through diet and lifestyle changes
4. Repair and rebalance: The right supplementation and lifestyle changes to start to heal the gut lining (leaky gut)

We work on all of these steps which lead to Vitality and then aim to keep this Vitality for life, not just to be healthy for a few months or a few years.

I like to think of our health like a traffic light system:

GREEN: Go, everything is functioning optimally, we have vitality, high levels of energy, life is fun full of joy, peace and happiness

ORANGE: Slow Down, you have symptoms such as headaches, joint aches and pains, lack of sleep, bloating, weigh loss resistance, aching muscles, PMS, PMT, menopause – this is your warning to do something.

RED: Your body has had enough, it is out of balance and you get ill with anything from a cold or the flu to autoimmune conditions such as diabetes and thyroid issues and cancer, this is your body's way of saying – STOP you need to change what you are doing to ensure a different outcome.

Our health is ever changing you can go from green to orange to red but you can always get back to green, it is all about the choices you make and hopefully after you have finished this book, you will be able to make the right choices for you.

DIGESTIVE HEALING

The digestive healing diet that I used and use with all my clients is based on a number of healing diets such as GAPS (gut and psychology syndrome), SCD (specific carbohydrate diet), the Gerson Protocol and the Paleo Diet. I am not saying that one of these works better than any of the others, I have included these to give you a reference and I find depending on circumstances each has its own merits, they are all based on a similar protocol of removing inflammatory foods, working on healing the gut and then adding in the right nutrients .

This is part of the Gut Healing Protocol we use at Kerry's Natural Health Solutions:
- Bone broth – this is really important for overall health as well as gut health and can be included as part of your daily hydrating fluids
- Include good organic protein such as chicken, turkey and wild fish
- Good fats such as coconut oil, avocados and olive oil
- Lightly steamed vegetables, using specific vegetables which are easier for the body to digest and absorb.
- It is best to avoid grains/seeds for several weeks but after that you can include grains/seeds such as quinoa and rice
- Dairy, remove this for at least 3 weeks if not longer, if you do reintroduce this it must be organic or you can use substitutes like homemade nut milks or coconut milk
- Improving the body's pH levels – one of the best ways to do this is to have ½ a fresh lemon in warm water every day, Breathe and add liquid chlorophyll to your water
- 1 tablespoon of apple cider vinegar in a glass of water 15 minutes before you eat is one of the best and most natural ways to increase the production of stomach acid

- Eat organic where possible and always wash your fruit and vegetables with clean water not tap water
- Pure water – not tap water – water needs to be filtered with trace minerals added. Tap water contains chemicals and toxins that can affect our digestive health
- A REAL food diet, this is eating food as close to their original form as possible, bone broth is extremely important when looking at beginning to heal your digestive system.
- Avoiding foods that cause inflammation and mucus forming foods
- Supplements are also important, the body is likely to be nutrient deficient due to poor nutrient absorption – important supplements to consider are magnesium (90% of the population is deficient in magnesium), Vitamin B, Digestive enzymes, and chlorophyll – these supplements are all important in the health of the digestive tract and ensuring that it heals and functions optimally. Glutamine is also an important supplement for healing the digestive tract and gut, bone broth is a great source of this and my preference is to get this via bone broth than any particular supplement

My philosophy is always food first, supplement second but in most cases we do need to "plug the gaps" due to nutrient deficiency.

Unfortunately, in this day and age even we are eating a diet that is 100% organic we are still likely to be missing nutrients. Food is picked when it is unripe, stored in cold storage or will travel hundreds or thousands of miles to get to us and fruits and vegetables start to lose nutrients from the time they are picked. Our soils are also depleted and so our food lacks nutrient particularly minerals, one of the causes of illness in the 21st Century is due to mineral deficiency rather than a vitamin deficiency.

When the body is dealing with any form of stress or illness it needs extra minerals and vitamins not only to begin to heal but to continue to perform its daily functions. Therefore, supplementing with the right organic, food based supplements can often be the key in improving and supporting our health.

An essential factor to consider is the quality of the supplements; I strongly encourage you to do your homework here. Supplement companies are not very heavily regulated; so in most cases there is no quality control testing from pill to pill, let alone bottle to bottle.

As with our food, supplements must be organic and food based, with many brands of supplements we are only getting synthetic versions of supplements (think again about "faux foods"), these supplements also contain additives and fillers, sometimes up to as much as 40% of the supplement itself, and in some cases they contain the incorrect quantities of some vitamins or minerals for example pantothenic acid - Vitamin B5 is an essential nutrient but added into a supplement in the wrong quantities it can actually cause digestive distress. Many supplements are not checked for things such as toxins, moulds, chemicals etc, if the individual ingredients contain any of these then it stands to reason that the finished product will contain these. We always need to be taking high quality, organic food based supplements. *See the resources section for more information.*

The supplements I recommend to my clients are actually allowed to be labelled "beyond organic" because they are produced to such a high standard. They are produce to a pharmaceutical grade, which means that they are regulated by the FDA with the same rigor as their pharmaceuticals. It also means that there's strict quality control not only testing from bottle to bottle, but from capsule to capsule. I only ever recommend product lines in which I have the utmost confidence and would use myself; I would never recommend any products that I would not use myself.

You'll find all the products I mention in the resource section and if you follow the link you will get a 10% discount on your order.

(Full disclosure: I do earn a small commission from any purchases made via this link)

IMPORTANT NOTE:
Supplements are powerful and can interact with medications. If you are taking any prescription medication, it is a good idea to

discuss this with a Vitality Health Coach (information in the resources section) or take any new supplements to your Health care practitioner, GP, Dr or pharmacist and have them double check to ensure you're not inadvertently taking something that is contra-indicated. Often people start taking supplements because they read or hear something about a supplement or it is endorsed by a celebrity. It is important to spend money on taking great quality supplements that will be beneficial for you rather than just taking a whole load of supplements that you think may help you.

I will give you my basic recommendations, these are supplements I think everyone should be taking but as always would recommend that you have a review before you start taking any supplements

Fish oil

You have probably seen all sorts of marketing about the importance of Omega 3. Omega 3s are essential fatty acids ("essential" meaning that the body cannot make them from other fatty acids, and we need to get them through our diet). Both Omega 3s and Omega 6s are essential to our diet, but our diet is imbalanced in that we get a lot of Omega 6s but not enough Omega 3s. The optimal ratio of Omega 3s to Omega 6s is anywhere from 1:1 to 1:4; the modern diet is closer to 1:30 and the Omega 6s we are getting are usually highly over-processed and thus highly inflammatory. A basic and easy step is to add fish oil to your diet.

As with everything quality is essential when it comes to supplementing with Fish oil. Many oils are taken from the liver of the fish as in Cod Liver Oil, but as you hopefully know by now the liver is the organ that filters out the toxins, so unless you know that you oils are from the highest quality source of fish it is probably best to stay away from them as they are not the best option. The fish oil I recommend comes from the flesh and is tested for all impurities as well as radiation. If you are vegan or vegetarian you can get your Omega 3s from flaxseed oil. The body will have to convert ALA oil in the flaxseed to Omega 3s so it is not something that I recommend unless you are very strictly vegan.

Benefits: If you are struggling with inflammation, immune issues, or don't eat wild salmon 2-4 times a week, I would recommend this. It's also excellent for pre-conception and as a prenatal supplement and is critical for immune and brain development so a great supplement for children as well.

Probiotics

Supplementing with a high quality probiotic is a great idea unless you are eating a lot of fermented foods (by a lot I mean at every meal and consuming a wide variety of fermented foods and drinks). Actually, even when you are eating a lot of fermented foods, supplementing occasionally is a good idea to boost the good bacteria, I would recommend probiotic supplements for a month every 3-4 months. Ensure you are taking a multi-strain high potency probiotics and not probiotic drinks that are filled with sugar as the sugar kills the bacteria.

Benefits: If you have ever taken antibiotics and didn't supplement with a probiotic during or afterwards, then you could benefit from taking probiotics. If you have gut issues I recommend starting with a low dose and building up over time. Whilst we do need to repopulate the good bacteria you don't want to do this too quickly otherwise you may end up with the same symptoms you are trying to solve of gas and bloating whilst the body adjusts to the increased levels of good bacteria.

Greens Drink

Do you love and eat your greens? I love greens, but I know that I don't always get enough of them. If you don't love greens then you are probably not getting enough. My favourite greens supplement is Pea Protein Plus. It is a great tasting, vegetable protein drink mix that provides a superb nutritious blend and is free from dairy, gluten and lactose. It also contains antioxidants, enzymes and. It provides generous amounts of 18 vitamins and minerals and is a good source of vegetable protein, as well as green and whole foods, it's a great addition to a daily green smoothie.

You can also add in a greens drink that contains Liquid Chlorophyll, it helps with normal digestive function and helps turn ordinary water into a great tasting drink that you can enjoy throughout the day and can be a great companion to your food supplement regime.

Benefit: If you don't get enough greens then this is the next best thing.

Magnesium
This is one of my go-to supplements. I call it my miracle mineral - why? For several reasons: it's the first mineral to be depleted by stress, it's also depleted by sugar consumption, and both of these are issues in our modern lifestyles. There are so many reasons for supplementing with magnesium: it helps with sleep, alleviating headaches, muscle cramps, anxiety, blood pressure, bone health… you get the idea. I am never without magnesium and it is the one thing I generally recommend to all my clients, everyone I know who takes magnesium has seen the benefits.

Benefits: If you struggle with sleep, stress, anxiety, or find it hard to relax (mentally or physically). It can make a huge difference if you suffer from headaches, especially migraines. If you struggle with occasional constipation it can help keep things moving. Please note that it is not a solution for long-term or chronic constipation, these are serious issues that need to be addressed.

You'll find all the products I mention in the resource section and if you follow the link you will get a 10% discount on your order. (*Full disclosure: I do earn a small commission from any purchases made via this link*)

ProArgi9+

L-arginine is a vital amino acid that plays a role in a number of physiological functions in the body. It is best known for its *cardiovascular* benefits, it is converted to nitric oxide in the body and it relaxes the blood vessels and regulates blood vessel tone and flexibility. It helps to improve blood flow, limits muscle fatigue and increases endurance - which in turn reduces stress on the heart, improves circulation and lowers blood pressure.

Nitric Oxide increases the O_2-carrying efficiency in the body, so it increases oxygen delivery to the body's cells, which helps with ph balance, fatigue and inflammation.

L-Arginine re-ignites human growth hormone (HGH) – the hormone essential for repair, fat-burning, building lean tissue, and athletic performance. HGH also has anti-aging benefits. The amino acid **l-citrulline** is metabolized extend the life of l-arginine in the body which in turn provides additional nitric oxide. It increases the effectiveness of nitric oxide for up to 20 hours.

ProArgi-9+ is the highest quality l-arginine supplement in the world, as listed in the 2016 US Physician's Desk Reference. The product has been subject to multiple clinical trials proving its effectiveness and it has a patent pending (expected end 2016) for its ground breaking synergistic nutrition.

Benefits:
- Higher energy Levels
- Better Mental Clarity
- Less fatigue – greater endurance
- Lower blood pressure
- Increased performance in all areas
- Reduction in body fat
- Increase in lean muscle
- Better immune function
- Improved sleep pattern
- Reduction in wrinkles and cellulite
- Skin health (e.g Psoriasis/Eczema)
- Feelings of overall well-being

ADDITIONAL STRATEGIES

TAKE OUT THE TOXINS
(also refer to Step 3)

Another important factor to consider is eliminating and reducing toxic exposure and we can do this by cutting out what I call "faux" foods, processed and packaged foods, it is a top priority when reducing our toxic exposure. These "faux" foods have toxins and chemicals added to them and we can reduce our toxic exposure by removing these foods from our diet.

For example have you ever made homemade mayonnaise? If you have this only lasts a week maximum right, because it is made with fresh produce that does deteriorate over time, but buy store bought mayonnaise and it lasts for years......... does this tell you something is not right? Real food goes off, it gets mouldy and breaks down, processed foods last what seems like forever because of the additives, preservatives and chemicals they have added to them. I remember in what I call my "pre vitality" days, buying frozen "chicken breasts" once I started really reading labels and being aware of what I was putting in my body I went back and re-read the label – do you know what I found I think only 20% of it was actually chicken, that is not to even say it was chicken breast it could of been any part of the chicken!!

Kerry's Natural Health Solutions basic rule:
If a product has more than 3 ingredients, one of them is sugar and/or you cannot pronounce any of them put it back on the shelf!!

Around about now you may be asking yourself what do I eat? The answer is simple eat real whole foods – vegetables, protein (organic meat if you eat meat and vegetarian or vegan sources of protein if you are vegan or vegetarian), soaked nuts and seeds and fruit. These foods should be eaten in the ratio of 80% raw and 80% alkaline. Remember that the food and manufacturing industry is interested in making money; they are not interested in your health and wellbeing. What may be quick and convenient for you now will not be quick and convenient when it comes to your health later on in life.

I get people telling me all the time that organic food is expensive and my answer to this is – you will either pay for your health now or you will pay for your sickness later on. The truth is if you eat organic you will need less food, you will be fuller for longer as your body is getting the nutrients it needs. Cravings are mostly driven by your body not having the nutrients it needs so it keeps making you hungry, so you keep eating in an attempt to get the minerals and vitamins you need. If you eat "faux" foods you are not giving your body the fuel it needs to detoxify, repair and regenerate. If your body has more wear and tear than repair, it starts to break down and this leads to an imbalance in the body and ill health.

TAKE ACTION
Healthy Navigation of the Grocery store and stocking your cupboards

Always shop around the outside – just imagine for a minute your grocery store where you go most often…………………the fresh food and produce is always around the outside of the store – fresh fruit and vegetables down the side, fresh meat and seafood at the back – next to the bakery which you do want to avoid and then dairy produce down the other side – avoid the inside aisle unless you are buying frozen fruit and vegetables.

Always buy Organic where possible, the best option would be to buy all organic from a farmer or farmers market, or an organic delivery service, but if this is not possible this is the best strategy in the supermarket

Chemicals from conventional produce add to the toxic burden in our bodies and cause inflammation which leads to ill health and disease.

REMEMBER:
Just eat whole, fresh real foods; and foods that have the least human intervention

Avoid the 7 Foods on the list that cause inflammation: Wheat/Gluten, Dairy, caffeine, Nightshades, Soy, Sugar and artificial sweeteners, caffeine and processed foods

Try and avoid foods with labels but always read labels, it may be the one thing that makes the most significant difference to your health – one ingredient is great – 3 is OK as long as none of them are sugar, avoid any chemicals, toxins, E numbers and things you cannot pronounce – your body does not recognise these substances either and they lead to inflammation, toxicity and loss of energy as your body tries to process substances it does not recognise and does not know what to do with - it takes up a lot of your energy, leaving you feeling lethargic.

pH and Alkalinity – What is it and why should you test it?

According to Dr. Robert O. Young's New Biology®, in the simplest terms over-acidification of the body is the single underlying cause of all disease. (1)

Our health depends on an alkaline environment, some foods are alkaline forming and some foods are acid forming. If you know anything about swimming pools or soil you will know that having the right pH is essential in order to stop the water in the swimming pool from going green and in the case of soil the pH balance is vital to the health of the soil and the plants that grow in that soil, this is the same in our bodies.

If we can keep our bodies in balance, e.g., in an alkaline state this helps our body stay healthy and gives us the energy we need all day, every day. Over acidity weakens all our body systems, and when we consume processed foods, caffeine, sugar, alcohol and foods that cause allergies and intolerances, this also creates acidity in the body. This acidity must be neutralized, as the body likes to be in balance (homeostasis) the alkaline reserves in our body are depleted and this leaves the body in a weakened condition e.g., low energy. As the body becomes more acid and toxic it is unable to absorb the nutrients it needs from proteins and minerals that we consume and this weakens the body's ability to produce enzymes and hormones, which then affects the health of cells, which in turn affects the health of our organs and our overall health is affected.

When we are overweight, this is actually a problem with acidity and toxins in the body, fat is actually saving your life! The body creates fat cells to keep toxins away from the vital organs as well as acids, so one of the best way to lose weight is to ditch the diet and rather detoxify and alkalise.

Water quality is also an important factor in alkalizing your body, water is not only essential for keeping you hydrated but it is also needed to help flush out toxins. With regards to the quality of water I refer to the experiments by Dr Masuru Emoto. Dr Emoto is a Japanese researcher who experimented with the crystal forms of water. What he discovered is that different forms of energy influence water's ability to organize into beautiful crystal forms or not as the case maybe with negative energy. (2)

Dr Emoto demonstrated that water crystallization depends on the natural health of the water, water from natural springs and healing water sources formed beautiful and complex crystalline geometries - like snowflakes. Water that had been distilled or polluted lost its inner order; its ability to crystallize was profoundly disturbed. You wouldn't want to eat dead food… so why would you want to drink dead water?

Understanding pH
pH (potential of hydrogen) is a measure of the acidity or alkalinity of a solution. It is measured on a scale of 0 to 14—the lower the pH the more acidic the solution, the higher the pH the more alkaline (or base) the solution. When a solution is neither acid nor alkaline it has a pH of 7 which is neutral.

Water is the most abundant compound in the human body; it is made up of approximately 60 – 75% water, with the brain and heart being approximately 73% water, so you can see how having poor quality water can have a profound effect on your health. Being dehydrated by 5% can create significant health problems as so much of the body relies on water to function, refer to Dr Emoto's study, and you get the picture of why water quality is essential.

The body has an acid-alkaline (or acid-base) ratio called the pH which is a balance between positively charges ions (acid-forming) and negatively charged ions (alkaline-forming.) The body continually strives to balance pH, when this balance is compromised many problems can occur.

It is important to understand that we are not talking about stomach acid or the pH of the stomach, this needs to be slightly acidic in order to break down our food and extract the right nutrients, if the stomach becomes too alkaline we can end up with gas and bloating. For the purpose of testing pH levels we are talking about the pH of the body's fluids which is an entirely different matter.

What happens if your Body too Acidic?
If you are suffering from symptoms such as constant fatigue, muscle weakness, cramps, difficulty holding breath, these can be symptoms of over-acidity and lack of oxygen in the body, most people who are over acidic find it challenging to hold their breath for more than 20 seconds.

How to test your Body's Acidity or Alkalinity with pH Strips:
You can quickly and easily test your pH levels by using pH test strips in the privacy of your own home. You can follow the link in the resources section to get the pH test strips that we recommend and use at Kerry's Natural Health Solutions. Whichever pH test strips you buy please always make sure that they are for saliva and urine, otherwise you will not get as accurate results.

- Normal blood pH = 7.4
- Normal Saliva pH = 6.8 to 7.2

If your urinary pH fluctuates between 6.8 to 7.2 for your first urine test in the morning and over 7.2 for your second urine test, your body is functioning within a healthy range.

Urine Tests in the morning should be done before consuming anything. The first urine of the day is what has stored in your bladder overnight and is an indication of how well your body is working and detoxing whilst you sleep which is why it should be slightly acidic as your body is getting rid of toxins and this is one of our detox pathways. First urine should be between 6.8 and 7.2

The second urine of the morning should be more alkaline and you are aiming for a pH of higher than 7.2

If your saliva stays between 6.5 and 7.5 all day, your body is functioning within a healthy range.

The best time to test your pH is first thing in the morning, test your saliva as soon as you wake up, before eating or drinking anything. You can also test about one hour before a meal and two hours after a meal. Remember this needs to be done at these intervals otherwise you will be simply be testing what you just ate rather than the how your body is responding. To test your saliva, you will need to spit into a dish or bowl and put the test strip into that to get the reading.

If your pH is consistently below 6.0 then you need to take steps to change this.

TAKE ACTION

I encourage you to start testing your pH today. Commit to testing your pH every day for a month to get meaningful results and then at least two days a week going forwards – You can download your own pH Record Card and start recording all your information.
Get Your Downloads - Click Here for Kindle readers or follow the Link : http://bit.ly/1IesejE

80% of your food should be alkaline, don't worry this is not as difficult as it sounds – alkaline foods are mostly anything that is green. Stick to fresh vegetables (preferably raw if tolerated otherwise lightly steam these vegetables and also include parsley, chlorella, and spirulina), salads, healthy nuts and healthy oils such as coconut oil and avocado's. An even quicker way to improve your pH is by juicing. We always recommend ensuring that your juice is 90% green vegetables, this will jumpstart your alkalising journey and start to put your health back in your own hands.

Another great starting place is to start drinking liquid Greens that contain Chlorophyll, see the resources section for more information or click here to order #ID 1810762 and start alkalising your body today.

The Health Benefits of Liquid Chlorophyll

Chlorophyll is the green pigment in plants that facilitates photosynthesis – the conversion of sunlight into energy for growth. Do you remember those in high school lessons? If not and you are like me that was just a quick refresher…….
Chlorophyll is the molecule that makes leaves green - it is present in large quantities in leafy vegetables and to a lesser extent in fruits.

Liquid chlorophyll prevents the clumping of red blood cells and increases the oxygen-carrying capacity of the blood; remember that most people who are over acidic find it challenging to hold their breath for more than 20 seconds.

Liquid chlorophyll has a number of health benefits:
1. It is a powerful antioxidant that helps to reduce inflammation within the body. Antioxidants also support the immune system, helping to protect against toxins and wastes.
2. Chlorophyll is a naturally alkaline substance. According to some research cancer cannot survive in an alkaline environment and thrives where there is acidity and although chlorophyll is not yet conclusively proven to protect against cancers, chlorophyll does bind with carcinogens within the gastrointestinal tract and eliminates them from the body.
3. Chlorophyll binds with toxic metals in the body to hamper their absorption and promote their expulsion. In this sense, chlorophyll supports the liver and is an excellent catalyst for naturally cleansing the body of toxins.
4. Chlorophyll is high in vitamin K – essential to ensure that the blood clots quickly when the skin in cut.

As is true with many things, in the end it's a matter of balance and balancing your pH is part of that. As much you don't want your body to be too acidic, you don't want your body to be too alkaline either so it is important to achieve this balance.

Our typical standard diets in the 21st Century are loaded with sugar and processed foods which hinder the body's ability to optimize pH and most people are likely to be living in a state of low-grade acidosis.

The solution to this is nothing new and is something that is advocated by most health, wellness and fitness professionals and Functional Nutrition Doctors and that is to eat a diet rich in raw, organic, whole foods, this ensures that your body is able to optimize pH, giving you more energy and improving your health resetting your body and allowing it to release any weight that it may be storing to protect itself from toxins.

STEP 2.1
HYDRATION

Most people are suffering from dehydration; as mentioned previously water is the most abundant compound in the human body, comprising 70% of the body. Even a 5% drop in hydration levels can cause a surprising number of symptoms, water is essential for vital chemical reactions within the body, for cells, tissues and organs.

As mentioned in Step 2 it is essential that we drink clean water, a common comparison that helps to get the message across is to think of a goldfish bowl, where the goldfish represents the cell and the water it is swimming in represents the fluid that bathes the cell. So what is the first thing we do if the goldfish is sick? We change the water.

This leads on to, if we are sick, one of the first things we need to do is drink more water, ensure that you are getting enough good quality clean water, the water you drink needs to have good energy. We have discussed toxicity in the body and that dehydration and toxicity often go hand in hand, water is vital to help the body get rid of toxins and this is one of the easiest and cheapest ways you can do this.

Having a water filter is essential, and depending on your budget this can be a filter that is installed that filters all of the water in your house, or a simple option is a jug with a water filter, most of these filters do filter out the good with the bad so I always encourage clients to add in Himalayan Pink Salt which has over 86 minerals in it, or booster drops. Another option is to get charcoal filters and alkaline mineral sticks that are portable and can be placed in any drinking water.

When we are dehydrated or lose water through perspiring, urine, menstruating and breathing, we not only lose water but electrolytes as well, and the body likes to be balance so along with the water it important to replace electrolytes along with water, so as not to cause an imbalance in the cells.

If you wish to read up on water and energy have a look at the work of Dr Emoto and Dr Batmanghelidj. Dr Batmanghelidj said 'Water generates electrical and magnetic energy inside each and every cell of the body- it provides the power to life'

Things to consider:
Please avoid drinking water out of plastic bottles where possible, most plastic bottles contain chemicals such as BPA which leach into the water, particularly if the bottles are left anywhere where they get hot, I know if you live in the UK, most of the time you may not think this is a problem due to the weather but consider where the water was bottled and how it has travelled, you have no idea what it has been through from the time it was bottled to the time you buy it off the shelf.

A lot of bottles are now BPA free, but my personal concern is what have they used in place of BPA? Whilst there is no point in stressing over every little detail just something to think about, I personally still think it is better to drink water out of a plastic bottle than no water at all and I do this if I have to but I carry around charcoal filters that I can add to any water bottle.

It is usually not a good idea to drink water with meals as this can dilute your stomach acid causing issues with digestion and can lead to gas and bloating. It is advisable to drink water in between meals

Consider the temperature of your water – if you drink extremely hot or cold water your body has to work harder to reduce that liquid to body temperature, if you are ill you don't want to add any extra work for your body so drinking water at room temperature, slightly chilled or slightly warm is a good idea.

Your fluid intake can consist of herbal teas (ensure they are organic and caffeine free) and homemade or organic broth which is incredibly nourishing and helps to heal your gut lining.

TAKE ACTION

Start increasing your daily water/fluid intake, at first you may find you need to go to the toilet more often as your body adjusts.

There are several ways you can ensure you increase your water/fluid intake:
- Set an alarm for every hour on your phone and make sure you drink a glass of water every time the alarm goes off; or
- Buy a 2 litre bottle (please ensure this is a glass bottle – see above), and make sure you finish the bottle each day.

Start adding liquid Chlorophyll to your water – see Step 2 and the resources section

I am not suggesting you go from zero to 2 litres in one day but as with everything build this up with time, start on at least 500 – 750ml and then increase that to 1 litre and then to 1 1/2 litres and then increase to 2 litres over a few weeks.

STEP 3
TAMING THE TOXIC OVERLOAD

When we are sick, our cells are sick meaning they are toxic. We all know what toxins are, and I am sure you are aware that these are in our food, in our water, our household cleaning products and our skincare products as well as the air that we breathe. We are being bombarded by toxins in all area of our life and we need to reduce our exposure as much as possible.

There are over 80 000 chemicals in production, with more and more being added every year. We spend £250 billion on "faux" foods which are full of chemicals and toxins, even our supposed natural foods such as meat and vegetables are full of toxins from pesticides and a lot of animals do not eat a natural diet, they are injected with hormones to ensure they have the greatest yield of meat. This is one of the reasons we always advise to eat organic or locally grown so you know where your food is coming from.

These are just a few of the toxins that we are exposed to:

Chemicals / Pesticides / antibacterial soaps / synthetic and harsh cleaning products / Nonstick cookware and bakeware / food that has been sprayed with chemicals, when we eat the food we are absorbing the chemicals / Animals that are feed antibiotics and growth hormones – these end up in our bodies when we eat the produce from these animals / Vinyl / Canned Foods: BPA is a chemical found in hard plastics and the coatings of food and drinks cans, it can imitate our body's own hormones in a way that could be hazardous for health. / Dry-cleaning chemicals / pollution / fumes / beauty products / EMF)

Bisphenol A, often known as BPA is a chemical found in hard plastics and the coatings of food and drinks cans which can behave in a similar way to oestrogen and other hormones in the human body. It is an endocrine disruptor which means that it interferes with the production, secretion, transport, action, function and elimination of natural hormones.

Toxins can cause inflammation which can lead to:
- autoimmune disease
- muscle aches, joint pain
- arthritis
- asthma
- bloating
- constipation
- fatigue
- food allergies and sensitivities
- heart disease
- low thyroid
- cancer

and the list goes on (dizziness, brain fog, skin complaints, food cravings, trouble losing weight)

Toxins and toxic overload have a very negative effect on our bodies. The problem is that the process is so gradual that too often we do not realise it has happened and often this is not looked at as a root cause of ill health. Our bodies are becoming overloaded with toxins, causing inflammation and cellular damage; this compromises our immune system and means that we are more susceptible to illness, anything from chronic fatigue to the common cold.

Our bodies are designed to detoxify, our liver is our main detoxification organ and we have a number of ways of eliminating toxins but in this day and age we generally have an overload due to stress and the amount of toxins that we are exposed to. Toxins are not good for the planet and they are not good for our environment or our bodies.

Virtually every organ in the body carries out some level of detoxification, the skin, the lining of the intestinal tract and the lining of the lungs are three areas continually exposed to toxins.

We need to eliminate toxins as much as possible, when the detoxification pathways become overloaded we end up with a build up of toxins in the body, many of these toxins are fat soluble and are stored in the fat cells of the body so the vital organs are protected. Many of these toxins can be stored for years, if not a lifetime, as the brain and the hormonal glands are fatty organs they are common sites for fat-soluble toxins to accumulate. This can lead to brain dysfunction, mood swings, depression, hormonal imbalances, adrenal exhaustion and early menopause.

It is not only the food that we eat that is making us sick studies have found that around 884 chemicals that are used in personal care products and most cosmetics are known to be toxic. It is estimated that women put over 200 chemicals on their bodies before they leave the house in the morning (face, hand and body creams, cosmetics, fragrances, hair colours, sunscreens, nail products and many more if you take into account household cleaners)

Many personal care products (shampoos, deodorants, lotions, makeup, even baby products) contain hormone disrupting chemicals and chemicals that have never been tested for their health effects. We end up putting these toxic products on our bodies and in our hair day after day and the toxic exposure is adding up. There is more and more evidence showing that chemical pollutants are contributing to an increase in chronic disease, 70% of what you out on your skin will be absorbed into your bloodstream. If you would not put it in your mouth you probably should not be putting it in on your skin as either way it will end up in your blood stream.

We are all exposed to thousands of chemicals in daily living, through the food we eat, our skincare and the environment these are:
- chemicals
- pesticides
- additives
- preservatives
- antibiotic residues
- hormone residues
- heavy metals
- carcinogens

The human body is amazing and we have various detoxification systems in our bodies which are designed to resist damage from toxins: skin, sweat, sneezing and elimination are all ways the body rids itself of pollutants. The detoxification "powerhouse" of the body, however, is the liver and while the body certainly has the natural ability to detoxify, it can only handle so much!

If the body is overloaded with toxins, this may be contributing to your illness and your body may need a little extra help getting rid of toxins which can be achieved through a 10 to 15 day natural and herbal cleanse, including specific juices and smoothies to give your digestive organs a rest and aid your digestion and elimination pathways. I recommend at 28 day a natural and organic cleanse that supports all of the detox pathways, I run supported programmes for this throughout the year.

I personally use and recommend Organic Skin care Products from Neal's Yard Remedies; I have a combination of homemade products and my favourites from Neal's Yard Remedies. You may have a preference but if not have a look at the organic skincare products here or follow this link http://bit.ly/NURLDb.

Depending on how adventurous you feel you can also very easily make some of your own to reduce your costs, the basics would be coconut oil or carrier oil such as almond or argan oil and then adding in essential oils depending on your needs. Tea tree oil is good for antiseptic use, Frankincense oil for skin care and boosting the immune system. Peppermint oil is great for massaging your tummy when you are suffering with gas and bloating. Remember to always dilute any essential oil with a carrier oil before using it, and only use 2 - 3 drops maximum these are extremely concentrated – it takes 65 pounds of rose petals to make 15ml of rose oil. Essential oils are fantastic but can also be dangerous if not used properly so please always consult an expert to find the right oils for you.

What we spray in our homes also matters – spray cleaners make fine droplets that expose your lungs to the harmful chemicals –

make sure you use products that are healthy for you, your family, your pets and the environment.

Other toxins we need to take into account are the Electromagnetic Fields (EMFs) from our wi-fi, phones, tablets and computers, televisions and power lines. We are affected more by EMFs when our cells are weak and our immune system is compromised, and if we have high stress levels.

TAKE ACTION

Identify where your toxins are coming from – download my **Toxic Household Checklist** and see how many ways you can start to reduce your toxic overload. I am not saying you need to do this overnight but be aware where the toxins are and over time put a plan in place to reduce the toxins and replace your toxic products with non-toxic options.

Call me crazy I did this overnight so it is possible but it is better to do this slowly over time than not at all.

Get Your Downloads - <u>Click Here for Kindle readers</u> or follow the Link : <u>http://bit.ly/1IesejE</u>

STEP 4
MOVEMENT

Physical movement either planned exercise or any type of physical activity is important for health and vitality. If you want to feel better, have more energy and look younger, then you need to do some kind of physical movement daily.

I am not necessarily talking about training for a marathon, unless that is some you want to do and enjoy doing but for most people trying to train for a marathon would put too much additional stress on the body. I recommend you find something that is fun and that you enjoying doing. Take a dance class or join a walking group, if you do find you get bored alternate the activities you do on a daily basis and change it up to keep it interesting and motivating.

As a personal trainer I could tell you how many minutes to exercise, how many times a week and what exercises you should be doing but in my experience the best exercise you can do is something you enjoy and will continue to do every day. Many people join a gym, or start running because they are told they need to and 98% of the time most people give up after a few months because it becomes a chore as they no longer enjoy doing it. Do you want to be part of the 2%? If so do something fun that you enjoy and will do every day.

The types of exercise I recommend for healing are relaxation yoga, stretching, Pilates and leisure walking. You can also increase your activity throughout the day by taking the stairs instead of the lift, parking further away from the supermarket, if you use public transport to get to work get off a stop early and walk, these are all easy and simple ways to add more activity into your day.

Not only can physical activity can help you manage and prevent a number of health problems but it can improve your mood as it stimulates various brain chemicals that may help make you feel happier and more relaxed. You will start to feel better about yourself, increasing your confidence and boosting your self esteem. Regular physical activity can also build muscle strength and helps oxygen to circulate more efficiently giving you more energy.

Stress is a factor in many illnesses and exercise can help to relieve stress particularly the ones I mentioned such as Yoga: Yoga encourages deep breathing and connects the mind, body and spirit, stretching exercises release tension and increase blood flow to the muscles; Pilates connects the mind and body which helps to manage stress more effectively, it also helps to improve flexibility and strength.

Exercise allows the free flow of energy through to all parts of your body which increases health on a physical, mental, emotional and spiritual level.

Daily exercise will help you to be more physically fit and give you a good way to deal with stress, both of these benefits are helpful when fighting any illness.

TAKE ACTION
Choose an activity you can and want to do daily, start with 5 – 10minutes a day - incorporate exercise such as walking, yoga, Pilates, Stretching and tai-chi in to your day. Exercising or walking in nature balances the natural rhythms of your body and is incredibly healing.

STEP 5
BREATHING

Stop and Breathe: a lack of oxygen causes many health issues.

Oxygen is the most important nutrient in the body; without breath we have no life. Breathing is an important part of achieving optimal health, it helps you to stay calm, centred and relaxed.

Healthy cells require a highly oxygenated environment and deep breathing is one of the fastest ways to alkalise the body, we have talked about balancing your pH, so this is an integral part of achieving optimal pH levels.

When we talk about breathing this is deep breathing not the shallow breathing that most of us are used to. Have you ever watched a baby breathing, their whole tummy rises and falls, as we get older we tend to shallow breathe – try this now – can you take a deep breath right into your diaphragm and not just a shallow breath that has you lifting your shoulders?

Deep breathing can relax muscle tension, improve your mood, ease pain and even increase energy, it also reduces stress. Anytime you are in a stressful situation or feeling anxious you will find that you are probably breathing shallowly - take a couple of deep breaths and you will feel relief from the feelings of anxiety or stress.

We don't think much about breathing as it is one of those things that we do naturally and automatically, but the problem as mentioned is that this is often very shallow breathing and not the deep breathing that we need for optimal health.

In most cases if we have breathing problems, these are linked to emotional problems and this is because we often hold our breath in stressful and anxious situations as a way of holding on to our feelings rather than expressing them.

IMPORTANT: This may be brief chapter but that does not reflect the importance of this step. ***Deep Breathing is vital to optimal health!***

TAKE ACTION
Breathing Exercise
Take a deep, slow, smooth and relaxed breath in, feel relaxed and then let it all out. Repeat for at least 5 to 10 minutes day
Slow = 8 to 10 sec inhale/exhale
Smooth = No noise through nose
Deep = Breath reaching the belly
Relaxed = Shoulders don't move

STEP 6
STAY HEALTHY, SLEEP WELL

Sleep is essential for many vital functions and one of these is our immune system, sleep deprivation increases the levels inflammation and infections and these in turn affect the amount of sleep we get and our patterns of sleep. Sleep may not be a guarantee of good health but it is certainly an essential piece of the puzzle for optimal health and vitality.

Sleeping provides our cells and tissues the opportunity to recover from the wear and tear of daily life, tissue repair, muscle growth, and protein synthesis occurs almost exclusively during sleep. Scientists have also discovered that insufficient sleep may cause health problems by altering levels of the hormones involved in processes such as metabolism, appetite regulation, and our stress response.

If we don't get enough sleep we go into a sleep deficit, often sleep is the first thing that is sacrificed when people feel pressed for time but they overlook the potential longer term effects on their health and even possibly the short term effects on their productivity. Often the affects of poor sleep go unnoticed but remember that all illness develops over time, you don't just wake up one day and you are sick, illness develops over time and results from a number of factors and insufficient and poor quality sleep can be one of the contributing factors.

In Chinese Medicine, certain hours of the day correspond to certain organs in your body, by following our natural circadian rhythms (our body clock) we can enhance our health and going against this rhythm can decrease health. Chi – is our life force and we have 14 major meridians and flows of energy (our chi) which occur during a 24 hour period. Our Chi consists of Yin (receiving energy) and Yang (expressing energy). Each meridian is linked to a particular part of the body, thoughts emotions and spirit, each meridian has a two hour period where it is the primary meridian.

This is what happens whilst we sleep:

9 to 11 pm: This is the time to begin to slow down and prepare for bed, it is optimal to be asleep by 10pm. During this time your Liver stores blood and begins cooling it down from the day, you need to be asleep in order for this to happen effectively.

11 pm to 1 am: Initial cleansing of all tissues takes place, cholesterol is processed and brain function is enhanced - the liver begins to cleanse toxins.

1am to 3am: The liver cleanses the blood and processes the wastes. This is a common time that people wake up, our blood sugar drops to its lowest point at 2am so if you consistently wake-up during this time, you may not be eating well, you may be stressed, overusing stimulants or you may be holding on to anger or resentment.

3am to 5am: The lungs are working for respiration, oxygenation and expulsion of waste gases. The lungs are associated with Inspiration and grief. Spiritual practices such as meditation are thought to be more effective in the early morning, due to inspiration (inhaling spirit) into your life. Many people who are grieving or experience loss have loss of sleep during this time.

5 to 7 am: This is the optimal time for your body to move its bowels and make room for the new day's nutritional intake. This is when we recommend drinking a glass of warm lemon juice to stimulate the bowels, get the lymph system moving and to help remove toxins from the night's cleansing.

Although this comes from a Chinese medical perspective, you can see how lack of sleep can impact your health, affect you energy levels and contribute to lack of health.

Illness and disease is the absence of health and the underlying cause of pain and disease is due to blocked energy, in Chinese Medical terms this relates to a decrease of the flow of CHI through your body. Balancing the natural rhythms of your body activates healing.

TAKE ACTION

Tips for better sleep:

1. Make your bedroom a haven for relaxation and sleep, having an untidy and noisy environment is not conducive to sleep. Having a quality mattress and cool temperature will also help you relax.

2. Sleep or meditation music can help you relax and can also drown out any noise that may be preventing you from falling asleep.

3. Your room needs to be completely dark, consider using black-out curtain or a sleep mask, we need complete darkness for natural melatonin production, which is a great sleep inducer and has other health benefits.

4. Using a diffuser with essential oils such as lavender, vetiver, roman chamomile, ylang ylang may help you relax and hit deep sleep sooner – this is something I highly recommend.

5. Dim your lights as least an hour before going to bed and switch off all technology, the blue light from TV's, computers, mobile phones etc inhibits the production of melatonin. You need to keep lights dim and read or meditate so your body can naturally make your sleepy hormone melatonin (the hormone that is produced as it gets dark out, and regulates sleep and wake cycles).

6. Cut out the caffeine and alcohol, caffeine may not only prevent you from falling asleep but it can also decrease the amount of restful sleep that you get. Alcohol may feel like a sedative, leaving you feeling relaxed and worry-free. But, as it is processed by the body it has a stimulating affect on the body which will wakes you up in the early hours

7. Exercise daily, but make sure to you do this several hours before bedtime. You can try some restorative yoga before bed to relax you.

8. Try a guided meditation: Get Your Downloads - Click Here for Kindle readers or follow the Link : http://bit.ly/1IesejE

STEP 7
STRESS

There is no escaping the fact we live with stress in our lives, nearly everyone experiences stress at some time. Stress, whether mental or a physical leads to changes in many body systems. It can be acute (sudden or short-term) stress or chronic (long-term).

Acute stress leads to rapid changes throughout the body, almost all the body systems (the heart and blood vessels, immune system, lungs, digestive system, sensory organs, and brain) react to meet the perceived danger which can be emotional or physical, real or imagined.

Chronic (long-term) stress can have real health consequences and should be addressed like any other health concern. Stress sets off a series of reactions in your body that involve the sympathetic nervous system, (this part of your nervous system increases your chance of surviving if you were to run into a lion) the reactions that occur in the body are as follows:

- Heart and breathing rates speed up and intensify this is so you could have more oxygen and nutrients available to your muscles for fight or flight.
- The bulk of your blood supply is sent to your large muscles groups to enable you to fight or run (flight).
- Your digestive system either slows down or shuts down so that blood, nutrients, and oxygen are not wasted that could be used for fight or flight.
- Extra glucose is released into your blood to give you a burst of energy,
- Your adrenal glands release epinephrine and norepinephrine into your system to increase cardiac output and increase blood sugar.
- Cortisol is released from your adrenal glands to increase blood sugar and therefore increase energy.
- The diameter of your pupils is increased to allow for more light to enter your eyes, so that your vision is more acute either for fighting or running away quickly on any type of surface.

These stress responses are beneficial and even essential in a critical, life-or-death situation as this allows all of the functions listed above to work efficiently during a physical emergency to get you out of harm's way. However, your body reacts in the same way whether the stress is emotional or physical. Over time, if your body experience's all of these reactions on a continuous, low-grade level due to continued and ongoing stress it places a strain on the body that may contribute to physical and psychological problems and lead to illness.

There is no question that you would need this reaction if you came across a lion in the wild, but stress is not always physical, it can be caused by foods we eat and can be emotional when you have emotional stress, the reaction may not be at the same level but the same reactions occur whenever you feel anxious, tense, frustrated, or angry (In other words - stress).

With emotional stress we do not need to "fight or flight" and the excess cortisol and glucose that are released do not get used up, our digestion slows or shuts down leading to compromised digestion and absorption and this is the common reason why so many people are suffering from digestive disorders.

As mentioned the foods we eat can cause stress in our bodies, gluten is a chemical rather than a physical stressor on the body causing vitamin and mineral deficiency – a loss of key nutrients causes a fundamental breakdown in the body's ability to heal and repair and eating gluten causes detrimental changes in intestinal flora (AKA gut dysbiosis) predisposing us to infection.

Stress can be immensely harmful to your health; Chronic stress, anxiety and sadness doubles the risk of disease, intense negative emotions of any kind send surges of stress hormones throughout the body.

How Stress affects your body

HEAD: Issues with mood, anger, depression, irritability, sadness and a lack of energy, swings in appetite, concentration problems, sleep issues, headaches, mental health issues, anxiety disorders and panic attacks
SKIN: Skin problems such as acne
JOINTS AND MUSCLES: Aches and pains, tension, lowered bone density
HEART: Increased blood pressure, higher cholesterol, increased heart beat
STOMACH: stomach cramps, acid reflux, nausea, bloating
PANCREASE: diabetes
INTESTINES: digestive issues, diarrhoea, constipation, irritable bowel syndrome
REPRODUCTIVE SYSTEM: lower sperm count (men), increased pain during periods (women)
IMMUNE SYSTEM: Reduced ability to fight and recover from illness

Major causes of stress included work, money, and relationships. Unhealthy habits can also cause stress and overeating or eating unhealthy foods can be a result of stress so it becomes a vicious cycle. Commuting to a dead-end job, being stuck in traffic, eating the wrong foods, fighting with a spouse, caring for children, treating disease, not having enough money – the list is endless.

If your friends are always busy and stressed, you will be busy and stressed – you become the average of the 5 people you spend the most time with – so get new friends who are calm and stress free, I know this seems extreme but I do seriously ask you to consider if you have any friends who drain you – you know the people I am talking about. We all have them in our lives, the ones who are always negative, these people drain our energy and make us more stressed – you need to figure out a way to minimise contact with these people as much as possible to protect yourself.

Negative thoughts can be sneaky, slipping in undetected, but they have a powerful impact on our moods and emotions. Over time, they will begin to take over our thoughts altogether.

Think about these scenarios, and see if you recognize yourself in any of them:
Your partner is 30 minutes late coming home from work, and suddenly the telephone rings. Do you immediately imagine the worst? Does your heart start racing at the thought of an accident?

You apply for a great job and feel excited by the possibilities. A few days go by, and you don't receive a phone call requesting an interview. Do you begin worrying about errors you might have made on the application, or whether your skills are up to par? Do you assume that you won't get the job, and resign yourself to a low-paying, unfulfilling career for the rest of your life?

These examples demonstrate how easily our thoughts can move into a negative place. Your constant thoughts of worry can spiral out of control. Your brain puts the body into "fight or flight" mode in response to the perceived threat, a distress signal is sent to the hypothalamus, the command centre of your brain, then adrenaline floods your bloodstream, and your hormones go into high gear, your adrenal glands release cortisol which increases blood sugar, this helps to break down fat, protein, and carbohydrates, and suppresses the body's immune system, digestion and reproductive organs getting you ready for physical action. However, we are not facing a true physical emergency situation and when these hormones are left in an elevated state they can become toxic in the body contributing to weight gain, acidity in the body and ill health

If you are in any of scenarios as mentioned above then the stress "switch" is stuck in the ON position. Stress levels are elevated and the body then becomes extremely vulnerable to disease. In our modern lives we are often overwhelmed with stress and anxiety and the body literally responds as if it's ALWAYS in danger!

The good news is that it is actually very common and millions of people suffer from stress so don't despair if you identify with these situations: There IS something you can do about it.

Strategies to combat Stress

The process of learning to control stress is life-long; managing stress will contribute to optimal health and Vitality. No single method is always successful, a combination of approaches is generally most effective so don't let your anger, frustration, resentment and hostility become constant. The stress response can be short circuited by practising mindfulness and having joy in your life.

Nutrition and Lifestyle Changes
A healthy lifestyle is an essential companion to any stress-reduction program.

Eat good quality protein (organic or locally sourced) and good fats at every meal with lots of leafy greens, good fats and protein ensure a consistent supply of energy to the brain to maintain a healthy mood.
Eat a variety of vegetable and fruits, seasonal, local and organic where possible.

Cut out the following:
- sugar: stressed spelled backwards = desserts
- refined carbohydrates
- alcohol
- Caffeine

Increasing intake of the following nutrients: iron, zinc, copper, selenium and iodine and Omega 3 supplementation is recommended along with magnesium which relaxes your mind and your muscles.

Eat slowly and chew thoroughly to give your digestion the best chance to work effectively and absorb the nutrients you need.

Exercise
Exercise is extremely important for many reasons:
- It can be an effective distraction as you focus on the exercise and let go of the stress
- Exercise protects the heart and may reduce the harmful effects of stress on blood pressure and the heart;
- Brisk walking even for short periods can relieve stress;
- Yoga and/or Tai chi combine breathing, muscle relaxation, and meditation while working the muscles which are all helpful for stress relief.

Emotional Freedom Technique (EFT) is a very effective way of reducing stress, whether the source of stress is chronic pain or a chronic disease.

Theta Healing can clear and align many levels of spiritual emotional and physical energies and relive stress of the *mind, body* and *spirit*.

Aromatherapy diffuser
A diffuser can be very helpful with stress, not only does is act as a mini humidifier, but you can create a scented and relaxing mist to create a peaceful and relaxing atmosphere, or add essential oils that are uplifting. You can also get them with colour changing mood lighting. Just fill the reservoir and add your favourite essential oil, I have included some options below and a link to the diffusers I use.

- Frankincense Essential oil: Frankincense has a powerful effect on the nervous system. It helps to soothe and relieve stress and anxiety and is traditionally used to help calm the mind and increase focus. It helps to slow down & deepen the breath, making it useful for stressful situations
- Lemon: uplifting and fruity
- Peppermint: cooling and refreshing - stimulating for the mind and great for digestion
- Geranium: uplifting and floral - stabilising for the emotions

Eliminating stress entirely is rarely possible unless you go and live in a cabin in the woods, but there are many ways to manage it and reduce its impact on your health. Don't let stress or your illness define you.

TAKE ACTION

I encourage you to consider as many options as possible, do whatever it takes!

Find whatever works for you, from deep breathing exercises, attending a yoga class and daily meditation to working with a professional for hypnosis or ThetaHealing®. The important thing is to find what works for you, something that you can do every day and make it a habit.

- Listen to music which can be effective at reducing stress
- Remove yourself from the course of stress if you can, if it is at home then try and get away from it for at least an hour.
- Make time for fun - this is as essential, put it in your diary and do something you enjoy
- Keep a gratitude diary
- Meditation or Yoga can release and ease emotional stress and tension
- Hypnosis may benefit people with severe stress
- Massage Therapy may decrease cortisol levels and some research suggests that the physical touch of massage can reduce stress
- **Theta Healing is very effective to help you manage with stress**

A Simple Stress Relief Exercise

Imagine your stress – imagine your teeth gritted and jaw clenched, now open your mouth, smile slightly and notice that relaxation follows. Notice that you cannot have a tense face with an open mouth and a slight smile.
Clench and unclench your hands, open them right up, do you feel better?

Smile and remind yourself you are amazing, you are unique and created to be healthy and not to be ill, remember you are worthwhile and that you have done good things in your life. Think of a relaxing time or place, close your eyes to help you concentrate and visualise a times in the past when you have been healthy and calm. Bring this time to the front of your mind until you feel calm and can see a white healing light. Open your eyes and take a deep breath, close your eyes again and think of a volcano erupting and blowing off steam, see this as a symbolic release of distress and let the tensions release and flow from you like the steam that flows from the volcano, take a deep breath and open your eyes.

Breathing Exercise
Take a deep, slow, smooth and relaxed breath in, feel relaxed and then let it all out.
Slow = 8 to 10 sec inhale/exhale
Smooth = No noise through nose
Deep = Breath reaching the belly
Relaxed = Shoulders don't move

Stop stress in its tracks, and start feeling better today!

Vitality+K 7 Step System

Step 1: Keep a food and mood dairy and do an elimination diet - the main allergenic foods to remove as mentioned in **Step 2** are dairy and gluten amongst others such as sugar (refined and artificial), nightshades, soy, caffeine and peanuts. You need to remove these foods 100% for a minimum of 3 weeks and then reintroduce them on a rotational basis to identify which foods are causing your symptoms - Food is information!

Step 2: Eliminate all traces of your trigger foods, become your own detective and read food labels to ensure that all traces are removed. The foods mentioned above "hide" in many other processed foods and under different names for example sugar can be labelled as sugar, sucrose, high fructose corn syrup and many other names.

Step 3: Eat REAL food - avoid processed junk and eat food that is the closest to its natural form, for example, apples are REAL food, homemade apple sauce is real food but once you move on to apple pies and apple tarts the apples are becoming more and more processed and less and less recognizable as apples.

Step 4: Drink clean and filtered water. Increase your water intake as you need to ensure that your body is kept hydrated, keep away from tap water and drink clean filtered water and herbal teas such as ginger and peppermint will help with digestion. Adding Phytolife, a greens drink with liquid chlorophyll to your water will help with your pH levels, with digestion and inflammation. Try to keep away from fruit teas as they generally have a higher sugar content.

Step 5: Ensure you are taking the right supplements to aid your recovery. You need to repopulate the good bacteria in your gut with a good probiotic taken twice a day for 2 months. I would recommend Pro B11, studies have shown that this has been helpful to 90% of people with IBS and it is the probiotic I personally use. It has almost 12 billion bacteria per serving and is beneficial for all **gastro intestinal conditions.** Omega 3.6.9 **Organic Oil Blend**

which helps with inflammation, **Magnesium helps** the transmission of nerve and muscle impulses which help reduce irritability and nervousness**, digestive enzymes which** can improve the function of the digestive system. **There are a number of other vitamins and supplements which can** assist with inflammation and are needed for digestion, absorption and to increase cellular health. One of the best supplements I have found is ProArgi9+, it is in sachet form (so no tablets) and contains Vit, B, C, D3 and K2. I always work with my clients to design a bespoke supplement programme for them and their specific symptoms and needs.

As mentioned in the supplements section, it is *essential* that you take great quality tested organic and natural supplements otherwise you could be making your symptoms worse – many supplements are synthetic, contain sugar and traces of gluten, are not tested and often what is on the label is not what is actually in the product.

Step 6: Detox - we live in a very toxic world and are bombarded by toxins in every area of our lives. Since World War II we have developed over 80, 000 chemicals that are used in pesticides, herbicides, as food additives, cleaning products, skin care and personal care products and more. We are exposed to these toxins on a daily basis and it is essential to reduce our toxic load and reduce the toxic burden on our bodies going forwards. Our bodies are designed to detox, we have many organs and pathways for breaking down and eliminating toxins but the bad news is that most of these pathways and organs are overburdened. We also need a nutrient dense diet in order for these processes to function correctly and if we are eating diet a of processed and refined foods we are adding to the toxic burden and not getting the correct nutrition to help our natural detox pathways.

There are some simple solutions such as drinking enough pure water, other beverages do not count! Avoid as many chemicals as you can, educate yourself, read labels and know what you are putting on your skin and using in your home. At Kerry's Natural Health Solutions we recommend cleansing 2 – 3 times a year and you can contact me for more specific help and advice on doing a natural and supported cleanse. I run online group cleanses throughout the year

Step 7: Mindset, Gratitude - Have you heard the saying "Change the way you see things and the way you see things will change"? We all have mental and emotional stress at some point in our lives and we need to learn how to deal with these problems and resolve any issues to avoid long term negative emotional responses and negative attitudes.

You can only have one feeling at a time. You can't experience trust and fear, if you want to trust but you are afraid then fear is still in charge, if you want to be grateful but you are still resentful about something then resentment is still in charge. Trust and there is no fear, be truly grateful and there is no resentment.

The exciting thing about this is that you have a choice, it is simple, it may not be easy but the choice is yours, choose wisely – don't be limited by your fears and beliefs – live limitless!

CONCLUSION

So hopefully by this point you have you noticed something about Vitality and Optimal Health …………….. I will give you a hint it relates to mind, body and spirit :

(Nutrition~Emotions~Thoughts~Movement~Environment~Sleep)

these all pave the way for Optimal Health and Vitality. You can't have one without the others. We need to activate our bodies own systems for healing and stop focusing on fighting illnesses, disease, stress etc. Do you ever notice that whatever you fight against never seems to actually stop, people have been fighting the "weight loss" battle for years but we are fatter and sicker than we have ever been – instead let's focus on Optimal Health and Vitality and the steps we need to take to achieve that.

*"When we find the connection between our thoughts, beliefs,
physical health,
and life circumstances, we find that we are
in the driver's seat of our lives
and can make profound changes.
Nothing is more exhilarating or empowering."*
Dr Christiane Northrup

SETTING HEALTH GOALS

When making choices about your health here are three rules:

RULE ONE: Be Specific
You need to state precisely what you want, most people don't know how to identify what they really want in terms of health, they usually are very clear about what they don't want and when asked to make a positive choice most people will choose to improve just a bit so they use words such as better and more

For example, I want to feel better or have more energy BUT this does not work very well as our subconscious, computer-like mind is quite literal and it cannot interpret that statement – what is better, a tiny bit? How much more? If you are not precise for example I want to feel 50% better than I do now, or I want to spring out of bed in the morning and have 100% more energy, the mind is unclear as to your choice and it will not be very effective.

RULE TWO: Pull don't Push
Your choice must "pull" to be effective. If your choice is lifeless and dull and does not excite you, you will skip over it and it will have little impact on your life for instance if I said to you, I just want to feel better how does this make you feel? Not very inspired…..? but if I said to you I want to feel at least 50% better than I do now, I want to leap out of bed and look forward to the day very day and be able to get through the day without an afternoon pick me up……..does this excite you, would you feel more motivated by the first choice or the second choice?

The second choice every time, can you see the difference being really specific makes….you have to truly buy into the choice you are making.

RULE THREE: Best Possible Outcome
 Always go for the best possible outcome, dream BIG: For instance it is not enough to chose to have "better health," because "better health" might be having less headaches or less bloating or just wanting to get out of bed every day, etc. Yet technically it might

be "better health" for you. A much more effective choice would be to state exactly what you really want, such as "I choose to live with optimal health and energy to leap out of bed in the mornings and do the things I want to do (be specific – do you want to climb mountains, enjoy time with friends etc), live with happiness, joy and peace.

Additional Rules to Live by:
- Eat real food
- Move around a lot and play – have fun!
- Be open minded to all the stuff we do not fully understand yet, especially when it comes to genetics, our micro biome (bacteria good and bad that live inside us), disease, weight, obesity and disease.
- Be committed and do the very best you can
- Eat a lot of vegetables, especially green vegetables like spinach, cucumber, celery and add in herbs and spices especially parsley and coriander and turmeric – add coconut oil, extra virgin olive oil or grassfed butter to your vegetables
- Don't drink too much alcohol
- Don't eat sugar, or artificial sweeteners: Sugar feeds bad bacteria, bad bacteria create cravings as they feed on sugar, you then eat sugar which feeds the bad bacteria and so the cycle goes around
- Stay out of fast food restaurants - you know the ones
- Aim for nutrient-dense food
- Grass fed beef / pastured eggs / low mercury fish
- Moderate starches and fruit – simple and easy
- Be happy, be grateful, be kind, and count your blessings
- Get some sun
- Leave the toilet seat down
- Donate time or money to charity
- Did I mention eat real food, play and move around a lot? (Just wanted to see if you're paying attention.)

We may not know everything, but we do know **some** things, but always be curious and ask. The one thing I know—with *absolute certainty*— (these are the principles I live by, these are my "rules" for the game of life, I teach them to my clients) is that they certainly won't hurt you and are more than likely to help you. I truly believe that 95% of all illness is created by our lifestyles, the food we eat and the thoughts and beliefs we have that govern our behaviour and even now the field the epigenetics which is very exciting is showing that we can in fact influence our genes, as Bruce Lipton says our genes are the gun and our lifestyles are the trigger. If you want to find out more I recommend the book The

Biology of Belief by Bruce Lipton, we can no longer use the excuse "it's in my genes".

1. What you put in your body has a direct and enormous impact on how you feel
   - Lots of veggies in organic butter or coconut oil
   - Grass fed beef / pastured eggs / low mercury fish
   - Moderate starches and fruit – simple and easy
   - Remove sugar

2. Meditate : the less time you have to meditate the more time you need to spend meditating
   - Relaxation : deep breathing
   - Comfort : make body comfortable
   - Passive attitude : overcome distraction
   - Concentration point : point of focus

3. Lower your expectations : when we have high expectations we have a very low tolerance

   People who have no money, no family and no plan are simply happy to be alive, the majority of us live in an amazing world and we are still complaining.

4. Gratitude :
   - Journal
   - 5 minute journal
   - Walk
   - Visit

TAKE ACTION

Daily practice
Be Positive : focus on what you have, create what you like / want, look for and see the solutions, create pleasure, joy and happiness in every day
Avoid Negativity: this leads to lack, complaining, criticising, fault finding, worrying avoiding

AN HOUR OF POWER:	20 mins meditation
	20 mins music & Exercise
	20 mins gratitude

REMEMBER : What you put into your body affects what you get out of it – your thoughts create the world you experience.

COMMIT for 7 days – upgrade your willpower and make this habit failure proof.

Vitality+K 3 Day Kick-start Meal Plan and Recipes

More of:
Green Vegetables
Red, Yellow and Orange Veg
Blueberries
Clean Water – not tap water
Oily fish
Almonds and walnuts
Avocados
Melons
Lemons and Limes

Less of:
Alcohol
Caffeine
Sugar
Processed and packaged foods

Remove:
Fizzy drinks
Table salt
Processed Dairy foods
Artificial sweeteners
Wheat, Gluten, Bread, Pasta

Health Habits
Gratitude Journal
Increase clean water intake
Warm water with lemon daily
Deep Breathing
Meditation

Cut out:
Skipping breakfast
Yo-Yo dieting
Drinking at mealtimes
Easting too quickly
Kick-starting your day with caffeine

DAY 1

Breakfast:
3 Egg Omelette – use Free range Eggs
1 cup of veggies of your choice – e.g., tomatoes, onions, spinach

Lunch:
120g Salmon on a bed of dark green salad veggies (spinach, watercress, rocket) with fresh lemon juice and extra virgin olive oil

Dinner: 140g Organic steak or chicken with a large mixed salad with apple cider vinegar and extra virgin olive oil

SUPPLEMENTS: Proargi9+ sachet mixed with water, first thing in the morning and last thing at night.

*TOP TIP: Sugar converts to fat quicker than fat itself

THOUGHT FOR THE DAY: Nourishing your body is simple, all you need is real food, clean water and the right supplements

MY DAILY GRATITUDE LIST

1.

2.

3.

DAY 2

Breakfast
1 cup organic gluten free steel cut oats or qunioa (after cooking)
2 tablespoons walnuts
1 cup berries (fresh or frozen)

Lunch
Salad greens with 120g chicken
8-10 sliced red grapes
Sliced red onion
2 tablespoons slivered almonds
Dressing : fresh lemon juice and 2 tablespoons extra virgin olive oil

Dinner
150g baked fish (2 tablespoons coconut oil, fresh lemon juice and sea salt and pepper to taste) bake at 175deg C for 10 – 12 mins. Serve with ½ cup brown rice and steamed broccoli.

SUPPLEMENTS: Proargi9+ sachet mixed with water, first thing in the morning and last thing at night

*TOP TIP: Eat organic where possible. Organic = less pesticides which = a cleaner, leaner body.

THOUGHT FOR THE DAY: You help yourself stay healthy and even improve your health with self-healing exercise – increase your heart rate, improve your agility, reduce stress and boost your immune system

MY DAILY GRATITUDE LIST

1.

2.

3.

DAY 3

Breakfast
Blueberry Protein Shake

Lunch
Prawn salad

Dinner
120g chicken breast with a medium baked sweet potatoe and avocado salad.

SUPPLEMENTS: Proargi9+ sachet mixed with water, first thing in the morning and last thing at night

*TOP TIP: Build Healthy habits to last you a lifetime

THOUGHT FOR THE DAY: Stress in your mind and body lowers your immune system. Breathe deeply and relax and keep your thoughts positive.

MY DAILY GRATITUDE LIST

1.

2.

3.

RECIPIES

Snacks
- Sliced apple with almond butter
- ½ cup organic greek yoghurt with ½ banana and 2 tablespoons of ground flax or chia seeds

Blueberry Protein Smoothie
½ cup of frozen organic blueberries
Unsweetened Almond or Coconut Milk
1-2 scoops of Pea Protein Plus Protein Powder
1 tbsp of Turmeric
Big handful of Spinach – fresh or frozen
Pinch of Himalayan Pink Salt

Whizz in a blender and enjoy!

Vitality+ Green Smoothie
1 scoop Pea Protein Plus
1/2 avocado
1 large handful spinach
¼ cucumber
Handful of blueberries
1 teaspoon organic virgin coconut oil
Juice of ½ fresh lemon
1 cup of coconut water or filtered water

Blitz it all together until smooth and enjoy!

Prawn Salad
½ bag of rocket
1 sliced ripe avocado
300g prawns cooked and peeled
Parsley
2 tablespoons coconut oil
Juice of ½ a lime
seeds from ½ pomegranate
Layer the rocket and top with avocados, add prawns, parsley and pomegranate seeds

Drizzle over the coconut oil and lime juice – serve and enjoy!
Spice it up: add a chilli de-seeded and sliced and a few cucumber slices.

Mackerel Salad
½ bag of salad leaves (rocket, watercress, spinach)
1 sliced ripe avocado
Smoked mackerel fillet
Parsley
Juice of ½ a lemon
seeds from ½ pomegranate
Layer the salad and top with avocados, add mackerel, parsley and pomegranate seeds
Drizzle the lemon juice – serve and enjoy!

Avocado Salad
2 handfuls of salad leaves – rocket, spinach, watercress
5 -6 orange segments
¼ ripe avocado, thinly sliced
1 slice of red onion
Dressing: 2 Tablespoons apple cider vinegar, 1 tablespoon fresh orange juice and 1 tablespoon extra virgin olive oil

Baked Fish
150g Fish of your choice
2 tablespoons coconut oil
fresh lemon juice
sea salt and pepper to taste

Place fish in a baking dish, add coconut oil and seasoning
Bake at 175deg C for 10 – 12 mins.

All Calories are NOT created equal - Focus on Quality
Food is information and literally talks to your genes and controls gene expression, hormones and metabolism. What you eat has the potential to determine if you will develop disease or gain weight. Eating a sugar laden biscuit versus a small handful of raw almonds can promote expression for disease. So choose a nutrient dense meal where there are quality calories working *for* your health goal!

WHERE TO FROM HERE

Hopefully this short book has given you an understanding of what it takes to heal yourself, your mind, body and spirit. I have not been able to go in depth into all areas of health living and achieving vitality but you have a starting point.

If you want to learn more there are a number of ways you can work with a Vitality Health Coach, this is the first step, if you want to take action and improve your health, understand how to improve your symptoms naturally, without medication then take action and send an email and we will send you details of how you can claim a 30 Minute Discovery Session where you will learn how you can reduce your symptoms and start to take control of your own health, you will leave the session knowing the exact next steps to take on our health journey.

Here's To Your Success, To your abundant Health and Happiness and I look forward to welcoming you to My Natural Health Solutions community

RESOURCES

For EFT Practitioners contact:
Association of Advancement for Meridian Energy Therapists for EFT : http://www.aamet.org/

Research on the effects of transcendental meditation
http://www.tm.org/research-on-meditation

1. http://www.phmiracleliving.com
2. M Emoto. Water Crystal Study (Japan)

Take your free Lifestyle quiz : http://bit.ly/1Ig3JTj

pH Test Strips for Urine and Saliva (100 strips) by Simplex Health: click to order

Any Supplements I have mentioned can be ordered here : Click here **or follow the link** http://bit.ly/1qVFRNu

Phytolife: alkalising greens Drink, you can order yours by clicking here:

According to Pubmed, alkaline diets may result in a number of health benefits as outlined below

1. Increased fruits and vegetables in an alkaline diet would improve the K/Na ratio and may benefit bone health, reduce muscle wasting, as well as mitigate other chronic diseases such as hypertension and strokes.
2. The resultant increase in growth hormone with an alkaline diet may improve many outcomes from cardiovascular health to memory and cognition.
3. An increase in intracellular magnesium, which is required for the function of many enzyme systems, is another added benefit of the alkaline diet. Available magnesium, which is required to activate vitamin D, would result in numerous added benefits in the vitamin D apocrine/exocrine systems.
4. Alkalinity may result in added benefit for some chemotherapeutic agents that require a higher pH. (4)

DOWNLOADS

Kerry's Natural Health Solutions – FREE Downloads
Get Your Downloads - Click Here for Kindle readers or follow the Link : http://bit.ly/1IesejE

My Recommended Reading List:
Psycho-cybernetics – Maxwell Maltz
The Science of Being Well, or any books by Wallace D Wattles
The Go-Giver by Bob Burg
Reinventing the Body, Resurrecting the Soul, or any books by Deepak Chopra
The Game of Life and How to Play it, or any book by Florence Scovel-Shinn
You Can Heal Your Life – Louise Hay
The Tapping Solution – Nick Ortner
Miracles Now – Gabrielle Bernstien
Delegate to Elevate – Sally Marshall
Secrets of the Millionaire Mind - T Harv Eker
For Business - Ash Lawrence
Treelite.com – the official website by Steven Horne for Tree of Light where you can access articles to learn how to change your approach to health. Steven Horne's approach to health and wellness resonates with me on all levels and I am currently doing further training with him to enhance my knowledge and to help my clients in a bigger and better way.

PLEASE NOTE : These are some of the books that have helped me on my journey, they are on health, mindset, thoughts, beliefs, business and alternative therapies. Even if you are not in business please do not discount the business related books, the actions, mindset, goal setting and topics covered by these books are as relevant to your personal lives as they are to entrepreneurs and business people, they might just change your life!

A Message from Kerry

I've been medication free, controlling my symptoms and healing my mind, body and spirit through my diet and lifestyle changes for the past 6 years. Prior to that it took 6 years of doctor's and specialist appointments, investigative surgery and months when I collapsed on the sofa at 5pm and couldn't move as I was in so much agony. Our social life was non-existent as I never knew when I would end up suffering from one or more embarrassing symptoms – fortunately I have a very patient and understanding husband, and although he had no idea how to help me he was always very supportive, patient and sympathetic.

My mission in life is to help as many people as possible to achieve optimal health, to help you understand that you always have a choice and that by changing the way you think, eat and move can have a significant impact on your health.

I truly believe that everyone deserves optimal health and that this is achievable, that we are not meant to take medication to heal the worst symptom you are suffering from, only to then suffer from a another symptom. I also refused to accept that I had to live on medication for the rest of my life so I took control of my own health and after years of educating myself, attending a lot of courses and spending a lot of time and money I would like to give you a new perspective on your health and empower you to take control of your health. The choice to take 100% responsibility and be empowered is yours will you make that decision? Do you want to live a limitless life?

If you want to take action and improve your health, understand how to improve your symptoms naturally, without medication then take action and email me at Kerry_vlf@btinternet.com and I'll send you details of how you can claim a 30 Minute Discovery Session where you will learn how you can reduce your symptoms and start to take control of your own health, you will leave the session knowing the exact next steps to take on our health journey.

Here's To Your Success, To your abundant Health and Happiness and I look forward to welcoming you to My Natural Health Solutions community

ThetaHealing® and ThetaHealer® are registered trade marks of THInK
www.thetahealing.com

LEGAL DISCLAIMER - This information (including links to any/all site pages, blog posts, blog comments, forum, videos, audio recordings, reports etc.) is not intended to replace the services of a physician, nor does it constitute a doctor-patient relationship. Information is provided for informational purposes only and is not a substitute for professional medical advice. You should not use the information for diagnosing or treating a medical or health condition. If you have or suspect you have an urgent medical problem, promptly contact your professional healthcare provider. Any application of the recommendations in this book (including links to any/all site pages, blog posts, blog comments, forums, videos, audio recordings, reports etc is at the reader's discretion. Kerry Madgwick, Afritrans Ltd and Kerry's Natural Health Solutions are not liable for any direct or indirect claim, loss or damage resulting from use of this information, website, email, report and/or any web site(s) linked to/from it. Readers should consult their own physicians concerning the recommendations in this programme, email, report or linked websites.

Made in the USA
Las Vegas, NV
04 July 2021